Critical Guides to French Text

C000274652

106 Stendhal: Le Rouge et le Noir

Critical Guides to French Texts

EDITED BY ROGER LITTLE, WOLFGANG VAN EMDEN, DAVID WILLIAMS

STENDHAL

Le Rouge et le Noir

Richard Bolster

Senior Lecturer in French
University of Bristol

Grant & Cutler Ltd
1994

© Grant & Cutler Ltd 1994

ISBN 0 7293 0375 6

I.S.B.N. 84-401-2137-7

DEPÓSITO LEGAL: V. 522 - 1995

Printed in Spain by
Artes Gráficas Soler, S.A., Valencia
for
GRANT & CUTLER LTD
55–57 GREAT MARLBOROUGH STREET, LONDON W1V 2AY

Contents

To Mandy

Prefatory Note

Le Rouge et le Noir is now recognised as one of the major French
novels of the nineteenth century, although this was not understood
by the first generation of readers. It was being printed in the
summer of 1830 at the time of the July Revolution which swept
away the monarchy of Charles X, and was itself a forceful political
statement. Contemporary readers were often perplexed or even
shocked by the actions of Julien Sorel and of Mathilde de La Mole,
and few or none foresaw that they would become two of the best
known characters in French literature. For many modern readers the
character of Julien Sorel has retained that power to disturb which
appealed to Gide, a great admirer of Stendhal. With its strange
blend of irony and sentiment, *Le Rouge et le Noir* is a challenging
and sometimes enigmatic work. I will begin with an outline of the
circumstances in which Stendhal turned to the novel, abandoning
his youthful ambition to write plays. This literary conversion, like
that of Balzac, is an indication of that growing prestige of the novel
genre which is such an important feature of French literature in the
nineteenth century. My references to the text of *Le Rouge et le Noir*
are from the edition by Victor del Litto in the *Livre de Poche* series.
The italic figures in brackets refer to numbered items in the
Bibliography at the end of this book.

1. The Birth of a Novelist

It was at an early age that literary ambition came to Stendhal, although he did not complete any works before he had reached the age of thirty. Born in 1783, when France was still ruled by Louis XVI, he was to live through a remarkable series of upheavals including the great Revolution of 1789, the rise of Napoleon and his fall in 1815, the restoration of the monarchy in 1815 and the Revolution of 1830. Service as a soldier and as an administrator in the War Ministry of Napoleon had taken him to Italy and Germany at times of profound political change, and in 1812 he had gone with the French army on its fateful invasion of Russia, had seen Moscow burn, and had survived the long retreat across the frozen plains. After the collapse of the regime of Napoleon, he had lived for a time in Italy before spending most of the period from 1815 to 1830 in a France full of political tension and ideological ferment. It is therefore not surprising that political ideas should feature so strongly in the fiction of Stendhal.

The desire to write fiction can come from the hope to win fame, the need to earn a living, the desire to influence minds, or from a purely instinctive compulsion. It can be the indication of a mind attempting to understand the world, or attempting to understand itself. All of these motives can be discerned in the case of Stendhal, and to them must be added a passionate interest in the great literature of the past and a desire to equal it. One day when he was seventeen he had noted in his diary that his ambitions in life were to live with an actress, and to write comedies like Molière. It would not be long before he achieved the first of these two ambitions, but he was to have little success with the second in spite of considerable reflexion on the subject. It is a matter of interest that Stendhal, although he applied himself to study the mechanisms and theory of comedy, never did complete a play. His case is strikingly similar to that of Balzac whose early literary ambition also pointed towards the theatre, before he discovered his true vocation.

This ambition to write plays can be explained by the low status of the novel, a fact which remained essentially the same in France in 1820 despite the impact of occasional novels of lasting European reputation, such as *Julie, ou La Nouvelle Héloïse* by Rousseau. Such major novels appeared like exceptional works which had done little to challenge the status of serious narrative poems, and even less to dethrone tragedy. It is clear from articles written by Stendhal in 1825, when he was Paris correspondent of the *London Magazine*, that he believed that one mediocre tragedy did more for a writer's reputation than several poems in the narrative form. Stendhal felt this to be the case despite the fact that the narrative poem was a genre in which Byron had acquired a European reputation. Comedy was increasingly considered to be a genre of lower status than either tragedy or poetry, and Stendhal had, by 1820, abandoned the ambition to rival Molière. One reason for this change of direction was his growing conviction that social and cultural change had made it impossible to achieve success on the stage with comedies which depended on the wit and subtle qualities which had been traditional in the past. The reason for this sad situation, he believed, was the nature of the theatre-going public of the nineteenth century, a newly-rich class which did not have the literary intelligence of the aristocratic élite which it was rapidly replacing in the boxes of the Paris theatres. Stendhal's gradually declining ambition to write comedy can be seen as a natural process in which his instinct led him surely towards the greater freedom of a narrative form.

The progression of Stendhal's vision of the novel can be observed in comments made in his letters, in his diary, and in articles written when he was a reviewer of books. Already at the beginning of the century he was becoming aware of some of the potential of the novel, though he had not yet been deflected from his ambition to write for the theatre. On January 21 1805, he recorded in his diary that he had read and appreciated *Werther* in a French version, showing admiration for the manner in which Goethe makes the protagonist express himself. A month later, Stendhal noted his approval of *Delphine*, by Mme de Staël, the first major French novel of the century. This work can be seen as a new type of novel portraying a woman in conflict with social convention, a subject which would be a prominent feature of several future works by Balzac, George Sand and by Stendhal himself. On February 5 1805 the future novelist noted in his diary (*3*, I, p.200) that he was moved by the misfortunes of Delphine, and expressed his admiration for the portrait of the aristocracy given by Mme de Staël. The decade which began in 1820 saw his growing interest in truly contemporary French novels, namely those which had the ambition to portray French society as it had become in the nineteenth century, whereas *Delphine*, like *Adolphe* and some less well-known novels, either set the action before the Revolution, or did not specify a time at all. In an article written in 1822, Stendhal praised Mme de Cubières for her treatment of the themes of love and marriage in her novel *Marguerite Aimond*, declaring it to be not only a perfect representation of contemporary manners, but also based on actual events known to many of her readers in Paris. Precision of social analysis and a story inspired by reality: this was already a blueprint for *Le Rouge et le Noir*, and we can see that Stendhal was now progressively moving towards his own formula for a modern novel.

It was about the same time that he was to feel most strongly the influence of an outstanding writer who was to have a major impact, namely Walter Scott. In his *Vie de Rossini* (1823), on which Stendhal was working at the time of his comments on the novel by Mme de Cubières, he paid homage to the Scottish writer whom he saw as an ally in the movement towards literary innovation (*7*, p.75). He noted that Scott, in his blending of dialogue, description and narrative, was making the novel into a more flexible, varied and entertaining genre. Stendhal's comments on Scott implicitly formulate a new concept of the relationship between dialogue and description, two elements of prose fiction which were not fully exploited by earlier novelists. He goes on to add that the description of nature scenes, which Voltaire had never thought worthwhile, had been carried to excess in the novels of Mme de Staël. When a description of a scene is properly done, he asserts, it has the important purpose of arousing emotion in the reader. The influence of Scott on Stendhal is of importance. Firstly, he provided a new and stimulating model for a novelist, elevated to the function of historian. Secondly, he created a new narrative formula which tended to make the novel form more varied, less abstract, and more entertaining. It is important to stress that Stendhal did not see the novels of Scott as a model to be copied superficially, as was being done by a considerable number of inferior writers, like the singularly untalented d'Arlincourt, but as one which could be surpassed.

However, the influence of literary models can function in unexpected ways, and it was not so much the example of Scott which prompted Stendhal to write his first novel, but that of a contemporary who is now almost forgotten. She was Claire de Duras, one of a number of women novelists who were a feature of the literary life of France in the early decades of the century, and who had been a prominent member of the salon of Mme de Staël. In 1824 she had published *Ourika*, a novel on the original subject of a conflict between love and racial prejudice. Encouraged by the rapid success of this short work, Mme de Duras next published *Edouard*, a novel which inspired words of praise from Stendhal. The French aristocracy, he asserted, had reason to be proud of this new book:

> I mean *Edouard*, a novel, in two volumes, by the Duchess of Duras. The incidents are supposed to happen in the year 1785. A young man, the son of an advocate of Lyons, consequently not a noble, falls in love with the widow of a man of quality. She returns his affections, but rather than degrade her in public opinion, by taking advantage of the weakness which would lead her to marry him, he embarks for America, where he is killed at the battle of Brandywine. His mistress dies of grief in France. There is truth and nature in this novel — nay it is said that the author describes what passed in her own family. (*6*, V, p.360)

These words are an implicit statement of his opinion about the sort of subject likely to interest the discerning reader of serious novels, namely the theme of social class. This was to become the basis of *Le Rouge et le Noir*, though with two essential differences. Firstly, the action would be set in contemporary France. Secondly, in a vital modification of the theme, Stendhal would make his lovers overcome the class obstacle, whereas the fictional characters of Mme de Duras did not do so. The contribution of Mme de Duras to Stendhal's vocation as a novelist is certain. He approved of her ambition to portray passion, an aspect of human nature which he believed to be lacking in many contemporary novels depicting high society. His interest in Mme de Duras was intensified by her next production, a story called *Olivier* which was not published because of its scabrous nature, but read to a circle of close friends who were sworn to secrecy. It was a tragic tale of lovers separated not by an obstacle of class or culture, as in her previous novels, but by the sexual impotence of the hero. When news of this clandestine work leaked out, the originality of the subject inspired Stendhal to write his first novel, *Armance*, which was on the same theme. Published in 1827, *Armance* was the apprenticeship of Stendhal as a novelist, and Mme de Duras had provided an important stimulus. Like her, his ambition was to write for that female readership which formed the majority of the novel-reading public. Is my novel dramatic and moving enough, he asked himself ? 'A-t-il assez de chaleur pour faire veiller une jolie marquise française jusqu'à deux heures du matin?' (*4*, II, p.97). Sadly, the number of readers of *Armance* was so low that the modest first edition did not sell out, and it is certain that if this had been Stendhal's only contribution to fiction, it would have sunk into oblivion.

Stendhal had now made the crucial move from theory to practice, and without the apprenticeship of *Armance* he would not have developed the narrative skills evident in *Le Rouge et le Noir*. He now had a concept of the elements necessary for a major novel: a contemporary setting; a serious portrayal of class; and a subject which was unusual but also credible. Chance provided the ideal subject on Sunday 22 July 1827. This was an event which was reported in *La Gazette des Tribunaux*, a newspaper read attentively by Stendhal because of its reports of real-life dramas. It had happened some months earlier in the village of Brangues, not far from Grenoble, his home town. At Mass that day, in the crowded church, was a certain Mme Michoud accompanied by her two children. A short distance behind her was Antoine Berthet who had once been tutor to the Michoud children, and who had returned to the village that morning. Berthet was well-dressed, of slight build, with large dark eyes. He waited, motionless and apparently calm, and when the mass-bell tinkled and the congregation was bent in prayer, he produced two pistols, fired the larger one at Mme Michoud and shot himself with the other. After a scene of panic and confusion, Berthet was arrested and was tried for attempted murder.

The trial began in Grenoble on December 15 1827 and was reported in a series of articles by Michel Dufflèard, a member of the jury (*2*, p.652). The courthouse in Grenoble had never been besieged by such a crowd, he noted, and entry was limited to ticket holders. This drama of love and jealousy had aroused the interest of many society ladies, eager to see for themselves a man whose apparently delicate body hid such violent passion. Berthet was the son of a blacksmith, but unfitted to hard manual work. As he was intelligent and of studious disposition, he was helped by some local people, including the priest, who encouraged him to improve his social position by entering a seminary and starting a career in religion. When Berthet had to discontinue his theological studies because of illness, the village priest obtained for him a post as tutor to the Michoud children. Berthet soon left this position, probably because of M. Michoud discovering a love-affair between his wife and employee. The latter then entered a seminary in Grenoble, but was considered to be unsuited to the priesthood once he had confessed his love-affair with Mme Michoud. Berthet now began to write angry letters to Mme Michoud, blaming her for his difficulties, and threatening to reveal their affair unless he received help. He then obtained a post as tutor to the children of a member of the provincial nobility, M. de Cordon. Berthet was dismissed after a year, apparently because of a love-affair with Henriette, the daughter of his employer. Jobless, Berthet again tried to enter different seminaries, and was refused. Blaming the Michoud family, he finally returned to the village and tried to kill himself and Mme Michoud. At his trial, Berthet claimed that his motives were love and jealousy, as he believed that he had been replaced in the affections of Mme Michoud by a new tutor. Because of strong evidence of premeditation, which he did not hide, Berthet was condemned to death. His appeal was rejected because of the spectacular and sacrilegious nature of the crime and he was executed on the main square of Grenoble on Saturday 23 February 1828, in front of an immense crowd which included many women. A witness noted that there was sympathy for a young man whose unpleasant side had been forgotten and who was seen as a victim of passion. Unknown to himself, Berthet had given Stendhal the elements of the work of fiction exciting enough to make a 'jolie marquise' sit up late.

The usefulness of the Berthet story to Stendhal was fourfold. Firstly, it was a real event, and therefore a work of fiction inspired by it could be defended against accusations of incredibility. Secondly, it provided a complete theme with a dramatic conclusion, and Stendhal was not confident in his ability to invent a good ending. Thirdly, a story culminating in an attempted murder in a crowded church was clearly a case of unusual psychological interest. Fourthly, it confirmed Stendhal's belief that real passion and energy were not to be found in the aristocracy but in the lower classes, which were neglected by novelists. The contribution of the Berthet case should not be overstated. The novel which it helped to inspire must be judged as a work of fiction, complete in itself. Although the character of Julien Sorel owes important features to that of Berthet, the essential interest lies in the way in which Stendhal was to adapt and alter the raw facts provided by the real event. The character of Julien Sorel, though not idealised in the manner of Mme de Duras, is more admirable than that of Berthet. Another major difference is the fact that Stendhal brings his fictional hero to Paris and into contact with the high aristocracy. This enables the novelist to give an important role to Mathilde and to other members of her class. The psychological enigma of the Berthet story is the inspiration for the central theme in *Le Rouge et le Noir*, a fictional work which uses it as a foundation upon which is freely constructed an investigation into the nature of love and of self-destruction.

2. The Art of the Novel

Stendhal believed that the first duty of a novelist was to entertain the reader, and that the balance between ideas and entertainment needed to be finely calculated. The essence of the novel, for him, was the narration of interesting events involving memorable fictional characters. It should be recalled that some outstanding French novels of his time had not given great importance to narration. *Obermann* by Senancour and *Adolphe* by Constant had concentrated on the moral and psychological aspects of the story, and these very serious works of fiction lean heavily towards psychological analysis and discourse upon a problem. This is clearly not the case in *Le Rouge et le Noir*, a novel with a significantly narrative character which is evident firstly in its very episodic nature. There are three main episodes: Julien in the provinces; Julien in Paris; Julien in prison. Within these larger sections there are a number of minor narrative units too numerous to list fully, which include the negotiation between M. de Rênal and old Sorel, Julien's first experiences as tutor, his journey to see Fouqué, the love-affair with Mme de Rênal, the king's visit, the visit of Geronimo, Julien's arrival in Besançon and meeting Amanda Binet, events in the seminary, Julien's return and clandestine meeting with Mme de Rênal, his journey to Paris by stage-coach, his entry into the home of the marquis, the duel with Beauvoisis, Julien's journey to England, the ball, the love-affair with Mathilde, the secret political mission, the second meeting with Korasoff, the courting of Mme de Fervaques, the pregnancy of Mathilde, the social elevation of Julien, the shooting of Mme de Rênal, Julien's trial, his experiences in prison, and Mathilde's last dramatic gesture. It is clear that this love of narration and multiplicity of episode is a major characteristic of Stendhal's novel.

An analysis of the episode relating to Julien's courtship of

Mme de Fervaques will throw light on the function of one typical Stendhalian narrative unit. In Part II, chapter 23, Julien is provided with a false identity and sent abroad on a subversive political mission. On his way to the frontier he meets the singer Geronimo, who consumes a drugged drink intended for Julien and who is consequently unable to complete his journey and perform in a concert. Julien does reach his destination, and communicates his message to an unnamed foreign dignitary who is involved in the conspiracy. He is sent to await a reply in Strasbourg, and there coincidentally meets another acquaintance, Korasoff. Learning that the reason for Julien's sad appearance is a disappointment in love, the young Russian nobleman provides a remedy. It takes the form of a complicated tactical approach intended to arouse jealousy in Mathilde by a diversionary action. The principal method is the courting of another woman by means of a series of letters, provided by Korasoff and copied out by Julien, who chooses the prudish Mme de Fervaques as the object of his feigned affection. Returning to Paris, Julien also takes advice from the Spaniard Don Diego, himself a rejected admirer, who provides information about the character of the lady. Julien copies out the courtship letters, carefully acts the role defined by Korasoff, and succeeds in regaining the love of Mathilde and even in arousing the interest of the unresponsive Mme de Fervaques.

This episode goes far beyond the basic narrative requirements of the political and psychological themes. The meeting with the Italian Geronimo is not essential to the story, nor is the inclusion of Don Diego, a new character who makes only a brief appearance. Stendhal, by adding Geronimo and the incident of the drugged drink and attempted interception, is continuing an old tradition of the novel, typified by *Don Quixote*, which made frequent use of journeys and of unexpected happenings along the road. His intention is clearly to entertain the reader by providing a variety of events. Similarly, the inclusion of Don Diego and the temporary prominence of Korasoff and of Mme de Fervaques show Stendhal's wish to exploit the very large number of minor figures present in his novel. The long procession of characters such as Chélan, Fouqué,

Amanda Binet, Chas-Bernard, Castanède, Frilair, Pirard, Falcoz, Saint-Girard, Beauvoisis and Altamira shows a creative exuberance comparable to that of Balzac, though even he did not include so many characters in one novel.

The episode centred on Korasoff gives priority to entertainment, and illustrates a conception of the novel as a flexible genre which is pregnant with potential developments, as when the nobleman offers Julien the hand of a rich female relative and a new existence in Russia. This detail is reminiscent of similar incidents in the semi-fictional memoirs of adventurers like Casanova and in popular novels of the eighteenth century. And when Julien considers this possible new road in life, the novelist opens up a vista of conceivable future events arising from the chance encounter with Korasoff. These narrative openings are a recurring feature of Stendhal's novel, and should be seen in conjunction with the major examples where Julien considers becoming a soldier, then a priest, then thinks of accepting a partnership with Fouqué, before becoming the secretary of the marquis. Other prospects are later considered, when Mathilde envisages elopement and a new life in Switzerland, when the marquis imagines the seducer of his daughter emigrating to America, and when Julien is elevated to an aristocratic title, only to turn his back on this new existence. Even at this late stage, there are suggestions of a possible escape from prison and a new life for him in a foreign country. Like these numerous fictional career paths, the Korasoff episode and its potential extension of the action into Russia is like the seed of a novel within the novel. It shows conceivable new actions which Stendhal playfully indicates in a manner which explains the great admiration of Gide for his novels. Stendhal's intention was to stimulate the imagination of the reader by means of a narrative structure full of possibilities.

The episode involving Mme de Fervaques performs a function similar to the one centred on Korasoff, for she is influential in the dispensation of high office in the Church. Like Korasoff, Mme de Fervaques is a minor character in whose portrayal the novelist cheerfully goes close to caricature in order to give zest to his satirical theme. The character is used to make a serious point about the excessive power wielded by fanatically Catholic women in the aristocracy, but Stendhal succeeds in making it extremely amusing. What is more remarkable, in view of the comic function given to Mme de Fervaques, is the fact that Stendhal also succeeds in the difficult task of making the character psychologically interesting. Mme de Fervaques is a typical example of a long series of minor figures who form an important part of the structure of the novel. The episode involving her and Julien is a brief departure from the basic needs of the main narrative and it shows how Stendhal treated the life of his protagonist as an uncertain journey over roads of variable interest. Indeed it is the metaphor of a journey which he uses when there is a comment by the narrator on the episode with Mme de Fervaques: 'Tout l'ennui de cette vie sans intérêt que menait Julien est sans doute partagé par le lecteur. Ce sont là les landes de notre voyage' (p.439). But the novelist certainly hopes that the reader will discount this ironical self-deprecation in a work which aims to entertain us with its numerous sub-plots and colourful minor characters like Mme de Fervaques. This emphasis on the frequent introduction of new characters and on the narration of new actions places Stendhal clearly in the great tradition of the picaresque novel.

The narration of scenes of action also forms an essential part of the main plot, as can be seen in the episode where Julien revisits Verrières and decides to enter the bedroom of the unsuspecting Mme de Rênal in the middle of the night. The novelist first describes how Julien buys a ladder, then he indicates the thoughts of the farmer who sells it, then the manner in which the protagonist gets into the gardens after surviving the danger from the dogs. Julien reaches the foot of the wall outside the former bedroom of Mme de Rênal, and is anxious at the thought that it may now be occupied by some hostile stranger. He throws pebbles against the shutter, but there is no response. He climbs up the ladder and knocks on the shutter, but still there is no reply. He gets down, moves the ladder, climbs up again, releases the catch holding the shutter after passing his hand through an opening in the shape of a heart, a detail to be appreciated by those who like Freudian symbols. He is aware of the danger of being shot as a thief, but sees a ghost-like figure in the room, and pushes on the window:

> Un petit bruit sec se fit entendre; l'espagnolette de la fenêtre cédait; il poussa la croisée et sauta légèrement dans la chambre.
>
> Le fantôme blanc s'éloignait; il lui prit les bras; c'était une femme. Toutes ses idées de courage s'évanouirent. "Si c'est elle, que va-t-elle dire?" Que devint-il, quand il comprit à un petit cri que c'était Mme de Rênal?
>
> Il la serra dans ses bras; elle tremblait, et avait à peine la force de le repousser.
>
> — Malheureux! que faites-vous? (p.236)

There follows a scene where the novelist gives the gestures of the characters with theatrical precision. When Mme de Rênal succumbs again and agrees to hide Julien in her room, Stendhal exploits the dramatic potential of the situation with a number of precise and realistic details. Firstly, the lovers must hide the ladder, then find a way to deceive the servants. The ladder disappears mysteriously. Can some enemy be aware of the dangerous clandestine meeting? Then there is a sudden commotion and Julien has to jump from a window while Mme de Rênal faces her husband:

> Elle alla avec lui à la fenêtre du cabinet; elle prit ensuite le temps de cacher ses habits. Elle ouvrit enfin à son mari bouillant de colère. Il regarda dans la chambre, dans le cabinet, sans mot dire, et disparut. Les habits de Julien lui furent jetés, il les saisit, et courut rapidement vers le bas du jardin du côté du Doubs.
>
> Comme il courait, il entendit siffler une balle, et aussitôt le bruit d'un coup de fusil. (p.246)

It is important to observe that this dramatic scene of action also

provides a precise portrayal of the complex emotional reactions of
the protagonists. What Stendhal has achieved is a successful blending of psychological analysis with the narration of actions which
succeed each other in breathless sequence. He has combined in one
novel the contrasting qualities to be found separately in those of
certain talented contemporaries, the physical adventures of the
heroes of Scott and the emotional ones of those of Mme de Duras.
This admirer of Shakespeare had now created a literary form full of
narrative energy. He had not so much abandoned his early theatrical
ambition as transferred it from the stage to the novel, while main-
taining some essential dramatic principles.

Stendhal's intention to entertain the reader is evident not only
in episodes like the one which we have just considered, but also in
the presence of a number of comic scenes. Some of these are
developed into episodes of a certain length and prominence, like
that of the visit of a foreign king to Verrières, in Part I, chapter 18.
In this chapter Stendhal describes the intrigues of prominent
families who want their young men to be chosen for a guard of
honour to be dressed in a fine uniform for the occasion. The comic
power of the episode is greatest in the portrayal of the Church. A
young man in clerical garb is standing before a mirror, apparently
giving benedictions to it, and the novelist carefully extracts the
maximum effect from the scene observed by Julien: 'Que peut
signifier ceci, pensa-t-il? est-ce une cérémonie préparatoire
qu'accomplit ce jeune prêtre?' The giver of benedictions is revealed
to be the Bishop of Agde, a frivolous young man obsessed by his
appearance. His first concern is for his episcopal mitre, as he
explains to Julien: 'On l'a mal emballée à Paris; la toile d'argent est
horriblement gâtée vers le haut. Cela fera le plus vilain effet, ajouta
le jeune évêque d'un air triste, et encore on me fait attendre!' His
other great concern is that the foreign king may find him not to be
sufficiently old and serious for his position, which is why he has
been gesticulating in front of the mirror: 'C'est clair, dit Julien,
osant enfin comprendre, il s'exerce à donner la bénédiction'
(p.122). Though the novelist uses the methods of comedy in this
demystification of clerical dignity, it is clear that his aim is not only

to entertain the reader, as the rest of the episode makes a serious statement about the power of the fanatical bishop to influence young minds. The episode of the royal visit and the histrionic bishop is an example of anti-clerical satire as funny and as effective as any written by Voltaire.

The scenes relating to Julien's duel with Beauvoisis are another illustration of Stendhal's comic skills. The episode begins with an encounter in a Paris café, very similar to a situation already used in the incident with Amanda Binet in a café in Besançon. This fact shows Stendhal's willingness to use repetition if he feels that it will entertain the reader, and the scene is a pretext for a satirical portrait of an aristocratic dandy who is contrasted with the ex-officer Liéven, another episodic minor figure. Stendhal amusingly places us inside the mind of Beauvoisis, who cannot understand why a complete stranger wants to fight a duel with him (p.289). The whole chapter which Stendhal devotes to this comic incident concludes with the paradox that a sort of friendship begins between Julien and Beauvoisis. It is one of the ironies of the novel that the proud plebeian is full of admiration for a series of aristocrats, including the Bishop of Agde, Korasoff, Beauvoisis, Croisenois, the marquis, and his son Norbert.

In addition to anti-clerical satire and to the comedy of class, there is the psychological comedy of the relationship between Julien and Mathilde. It is from the time she begins an exchange of letters with Julien that the humour of the situation is developed. For example in the wording of the note in which Mathilde invites him to her bedroom at midnight: 'J'ai besoin de vous parler; il faut que je vous parle, ce soir; au moment où une heure après minuit sonnera, trouvez-vous dans le jardin. Prenez la grande échelle du jardinier auprès du puits; placez-la contre ma fenêtre et montez chez moi. Il fait clair de lune; n'importe' (p.354). Because he fears a trap, Julien is holding a pistol when he climbs the ladder to enter the room. Then comes an extraordinary seduction scene the originality of which lies in the blending of parodic elements with a psychological portrayal which has its own coherence and logic, given the unusual nature of Mathilde. It is she who directs the preparation for her own

seduction, in a manner which shows her radical difference from the
unworldly heroines of Mme de Duras:

> — Il faut abaisser l'échelle, dit Mathilde.
> — Elle est immense, et peut casser les vitres du salon en
> bas, ou de l'entresol.
> — Il ne faut pas casser les vitres, reprit Mathilde
> essayant en vain de prendre le ton de la conversation
> ordinaire; vous pourriez, ce me semble, abaisser
> l'échelle au moyen d'une corde qu'on attacherait au
> premier échelon. J'ai toujours une provision de cordes
> chez moi. (pp.361–62)

The resourceful Mathilde with her supply of ropes is less able to
cope with the emotional implications of the situation, and Julien is
still anxious about possible enemies under the bed. One source of
comedy in this scene is the fact that both characters are playing a
role which is conventional, as the novelist ironically reinvents the
fictional tradition of the love-scene. And by having Julien make up
for his lack of sincere emotion by quoting from *La Nouvelle
Héloïse*, Stendhal makes his parodic intention explicit. Julien uses
the traditional discourse of love, but emptied of its essential ingredi-
ent. This is not parody for its own sake, as the type of comedy here
created by Stendhal has a similarity to that based on anti-clerical
satire and on the theme of social class. The aim of the novelist is a
serious one in this case too, as the strange behaviour of Mathilde is
intended to illustrate an interesting psychological phenomenon, the
interference of literary models with reality. The question of the
novelist's attitude to this role-playing by Julien and Mathilde is a
complex one to which I shall return.

Verbal humour and wit are another significant element in
Stendhal's strategy of entertainment. Brevity and understatement
are a frequent feature of this humour, as when Julien is impressed
by the 'magnificence pieuse' of a bishop's palace (p.224).
Sometimes the humour has a framework of one sprightly sentence,
as when Julien awaits execution and his confessor, urging him to

reconcile himself with the church, says: 'Les larmes que votre conversion fera répandre annuleront l'effet corrosif de dix éditions des œuvres impies de Voltaire' (p.538). Explaining that Mme de Rênal found her husband less boring than the other men of the little town, the novelist allows himself two sentences of comment: 'Ce jugement conjugal était raisonnable. Le maire de Verrières devait une réputation d'esprit et surtout de bon ton à une demi-douzaine de plaisanteries dont il avait hérité d'un oncle' (p.25). He adds that M. de Rênal found it increasingly hard to remember these anecdotes, and consequently used them only on big occasions. Stendhal is most amusing on the theme of religious fanaticism, as in the summary of the education of Mme de Rênal where his concision and polish remind one strongly of the anti-clerical wit of Laclos.

A striking feature of Stendhal's narrative method is his use of interventions by a voice which at times seems to be that of a fictional narrator but more usually that of the author. These intercalated comments are used sometimes as a source of humour and irony, and sometimes for the communication of information of a different nature. At the time when Stendhal was writing, the old fictional device of a narrator, used by Diderot, and also by Sterne, by Fielding, and by Scott, was still common in many French novels. It can now be seen as one of the most dominant characteristics in the novel genre, one which went out of fashion under the influence of realism and naturalism only to make a strong return in the works of many novelists of the twentieth century, including Gide, Proust and Céline. *Le Rouge et le Noir* begins with the device of a notional traveller who is imagined to be visiting Verrières and describing what he sees as he progresses along the street. Then we are given more explicit information about the narrator who is to accompany the reader on the fictional journey: 'Combien de fois, songeant aux bals de Paris abandonnés la veille, et la poitrine appuyée contre ces grands blocs de pierre d'un beau gris tirant sur le bleu, mes regards ont plongé dans la vallée du Doubs!' (pp.17–18). It is gradually revealed that this traveller from Paris has thoughts about provincial life to communicate to the reader, and that he sees unis explanatory discourse as an important part of the story he is telling.

There are also a significant number of interventions made in an ironical mode which many of Stendhal's first readers found less easy to decode, like the comment on the hero's pretence of piety while he is still in the village of Verrières: 'Il ne faut pas trop mal augurer de Julien; il inventait correctement les paroles d'une hypocrisie cauteleuse et prudente. Ce n'est pas mal à son âge' (p.60). In reality, Stendhal's intention in this sentence is to denounce hypocrisy. There are cases of authorial intervention where the irony is more difficult to penetrate, for example the whole page of comment which begins: 'Cette page nuira de plus d'une façon au malheureux auteur. Les âmes glacées l'accuseront d'indécence' (p.380). This defensive passage includes a metaphor which would become famous: 'Hé, monsieur, un roman est un miroir qui se promène sur une grande route. Tantôt il reflète à vos yeux l'azur des cieux, tantôt la fange des bourbiers de la route. Et l'homme qui porte le miroir dans sa hotte sera par vous accusé d'être immoral!' The purpose of this long and enigmatic intervention is apparently to disarm the objections of readers who may accuse the creator of Mathilde of encouraging women to seek sexual liberation.

In addition to such ironical interventions there is another recurring type of authorial comment which is essentially playful in manner, as in the retrospective explanation of the changing relationship between Julien and the marquis, shown in the way in which they speak to each other: 'Le lecteur est peut-être surpris de ce ton libre et presque amical; nous avons oublié de dire que, depuis six semaines, le marquis était retenu chez lui par une attaque de goutte' (p.294). Indeed this 'ton libre et presque amical' can be seen as a good description of the narrative method which Stendhal adopts for the reader, often preferring the easy manner of an oral account which allows itself a certain looseness of structure in matters of detail. Another example of this nonchalant method can be seen in a curious intervention by the narrator at a time when Julien's life is nearing its certain end, and yet we are given thoughts about a future which is purely hypothetical:

Il était encore bien jeune; mais suivant moi, ce fut une
belle plante. Au lieu de marcher du tendre au rusé,
comme la plupart des hommes, l'âge lui eût donné la
bonté facile à s'attendrir, il se fût guéri d'une méfiance
folle...Mais à quoi bon ces vaines prédictions?
(pp.490–91)

The numerous comments of this irrepressible *moi* who bears no
name other than that of Stendhal, itself fictional and created by the
real Henri Beyle, endow the narrative with characteristics which can
be described either as defects or as qualities. On the one hand they
can be criticised as authorial self-consciousness, a sort of indisci-
pline, and a breaking of the illusion of reality. On the other, they
can be seen as a sophisticated game, as a means of creating a
complicity between author and reader, of not imposing fictional
illusion as an absolute end in itself, but seeing it as one literary
element among others. The communication of ideas is at times
given priority over the actions of Julien, Mathilde and Mme de
Rênal. Stendhal's interventions, though unnecessary to the action,
have the effect of occasionally distancing us from the story, with its
power to amuse, excite and to move us, and by this distancing to
encourage us to respond also in an intellectual manner to the
experiences of these characters of whose fictional status we are at
times forcefully reminded.

In spite of interventions which tend to inform us that what we
are reading is fiction, it remains true that the general strategy of
Stendhal was to create an illusion of reality. Physical description
was a dimension of prose fiction which he used sparingly, and some
hand-written notes on his own copy of *Le Rouge et le Noir* show
that he believed that his novel would have gained from a greater
provision of physical portraits of some minor characters and some
surroundings. It is the case, nevertheless, that most of his characters
are given some physical traits, as one can see in this brief portrait of
Mme de Rênal: 'C'était une femme grande, bien faite, qui avait été
la beauté du pays, comme on dit dans ces montagnes. Elle avait un

certain air de simplicité, et de la jeunesse dans la démarche; aux
yeux d'un Parisien, cette grâce naïve, pleine d'innocence et de
vivacité, serait même allée jusqu'à rappeler des idées de douce
volupté' (pp.24–25). The portrait of Mathilde as seen by Julien
shows Stendhal in his most skilful mode:

> Presque en même temps, il aperçut une jeune personne,
> extrêmement blonde et fort bien faite, qui vint s'asseoir
> vis-à-vis de lui. Elle ne lui plut point; cependant en la
> regardant attentivement, il pensa qu'il n'avait jamais vu
> des yeux aussi beaux; mais ils annonçaient une grande
> froideur d'âme. Par la suite, Julien trouva qu'ils avaient
> l'expression de l'ennui qui examine, mais qui se
> souvient de l'obligation d'être imposant. (p.265)

Here the number of physical characteristics is small, and the
novelist concentrates on the eyes because they communicate the
psychological attributes which are essential to him. Typically, he
does not inform us of the colour of these eyes, limiting himself to
telling us later that they sparkle with intelligence and wit. In spite of
its brevity, this portrait of Mathilde seems admirably sufficient in its
concision.

It is in the creation of natural settings that Stendhal's novel is
most clearly divergent from the new trend towards detailed description. It is true that *Le Rouge et le Noir* begins with a sketch of the
fictional town of Verrières, and here Stendhal has applied himself to
the task of giving an outline not only of the physical setting with the
white houses set in the wooded mountain valley, but also of an
economic dimension in the form of saw-mills and nail factories.
Such concern for portrayal of the environment is not often present
in the rest of the novel, in spite of the fact that Julien travels to
Besançon, Paris, England, Strasbourg and elsewhere. These
journeys would have been used by Balzac and other contemporaries
in order to introduce descriptions. However, many modern readers,
whose imaginative response to verbal description has probably been
blunted by a culture saturated by pictures of all types, find that the

few descriptions actually provided by Stendhal have an impact which is greater because of their rarity.

This was not the opinion of Zola, who declared in *Les Romanciers naturalistes* that a lack of description of the physical environment was a serious shortcoming in Stendhal. To back up this claim, he referred to the episode in which Julien takes the hand of Mme de Rênal. If this interesting scene had been given to a natural- ist novelist, asserted Zola, he would have narrated it better by showing the physiological influence of the surroundings on the heroine: 'Donnez l'épisode à un écrivain pour qui les milieux existent, et dans la défaite de cette femme, il fera entrer la nuit, avec ses odeurs, avec ses voix, avec ses voluptés molles. Et cet écrivain sera dans la vérité, son tableau sera plus complet' (*41*, p.89). The injustice of Zola's criticism is revealed by a careful reading of the actual episode, which will show that Stendhal does indeed provide a description of the physical setting, but reduced to a minimum. His method is to evoke it only in so far as it is relevant to the thoughts and emotions of the characters.

The finest example of a Stendhalian description of a natural scene is probably the one in which Julien has escaped momentarily from the constraints of his social situation, and is enjoying a rare experience of liberty and exaltation in the Romantic setting of a mountain top:

> Julien, debout sur son grand rocher, regardait le ciel, embrasé par un soleil d'août. Les cigales chantaient dans le champ au-dessous du rocher; quand elles se taisaient tout était silence autour de lui. Il voyait à ses pieds vingt lieues de pays. Quelque épervier parti des grandes roches au-dessus de sa tête était aperçu par lui, de temps à autre, décrivant en silence ses cercles immenses. L'œil de Julien suivait machinalement l'oiseau de proie. Ses mouvements tranquilles et puissants le frappaient, il enviait cette force, il enviait

cet isolement.

C'était la destinée de Napoléon, serait-ce un jour la
sienne? (p.77)

Once again, the first characteristic of the description is economy.
Stendhal reduces the elements to a vital few: the rock, the sun, the
crickets, the vista, the solitary bird of prey which dominates the
scene, and to which is given an explicit symbolic significance. And
once again, it is the brevity of the description which makes it easier
for us to create the scene freely in our own imagination because it is
not constrained by a mass of information.

We have here an illustration of a literary principle formulated
by Stendhal in *Vie de Henry Brulard* by means of another metaphor
which would become well known: 'Un roman est comme un archet,
la caisse du violon qui *rend les sons* c'est l'âme du lecteur' (*3*, II,
p.699). This concept of literature has important implications: firstly,
the literary text is but one part of a performance. It is of course
fundamental, but it is no more than an instrument designed to
perform a function, and its quality resides in the performance and
not in some abstract dimension. Just as a good performer on the
violin will not make unnecessary flourishes with the bow, Stendhal
concentrates on the essential. With a minimum of words, and by
using free indirect style in the last two sentences, he achieves not
only a description of the natural scene, but also, and principally, a
portrayal of the mind of Julien. As the narrative slides easily from
an objective perspective into the angle of vision of Julien, we are
shown not only the object observed, but also the observer. This
subtle and economical narrative method, which would later become
widespread in the French novel, is an important part of Stendhal's
modernity. It must be remembered that economy of style was
unfashionable with the majority of Stendhal's contemporaries, and
that he was later to remark that if *La Chartreuse de Parme* had been
written by George Sand, it would have sold more copies, but there
would have been three volumes instead of two.

Another salient feature of Stendhal's narrative method is his
portrayal of states of mind by interior monologue, a procedure

which he did not invent but which he developed. Interior monologue in novels can be seen as a sophisticated adaptation of the type of simple soliloquy used in plays and in narrative poems. Stendhal uses it most frequently for Julien, but does not limit it to his major characters. The result is that we are presented with a plurality of viewpoints which at times can be surprising, when he views the world through the eyes of characters which have not previously been portrayed with sympathy. A good example of this can be found where M. de Rênal reacts to an anonymous letter accusing his wife of adultery. For a considerable part of this chapter the novelist places us inside the mind of this minor character as he speculates indecisively about possible action. The interior monologue skilfully reveals the mental processes and the personality of a man torn between an instinct which tells him to turn a blind eye, and a desire for vengeance:

> "Grâce au ciel, disait M. de Rênal dans d'autres moments, je n'ai point de fille, et la façon dont je vais punir la mère ne nuira point à l'établissement de mes enfants; je puis surprendre ce petit paysan avec ma femme et les tuer tous les deux; dans ce cas, le tragique de l'aventure en ôtera peut-être le ridicule. Cette idée lui sourit; il la suivit dans tous ses détails. Le code pénal est pour moi, et, quoi qu'il arrive, notre congrégation et mes amis du jury me sauveront." Il examina son couteau de chasse qui était fort tranchant; mais l'idée du sang lui fit peur. (p.143)

Stendhal's method here is a fusion of interior monologue and of authorial comment. The transition from the thoughts of the character into the narrative mode, and back again, is achieved with lightness of touch. This nimble and effortless method used for the portrayal of the evolving psychological state of a character was one of Stendhal's significant contributions to the French novel.

The advantage of interior monologue, used in this way, is not only elegance and economy, but also an illusion of psychological reality, as the author gives us the impression that we are in direct contact with the thoughts of the character. Another striking example of interior monologue can be found in part II, chapter 8, where the novelist communicates the thoughts of Mathilde as she assesses the men of her social milieu. What Stendhal gives us in this case is a reasoning process, taking place in the mind of the character but which contains ideas shared by the author, who transfers to Mathilde the important task of formulating them. Preferring at times to be a discreet persuader, Stendhal has recourse to this indirect method of communication, but only by using a few privileged fictional characters. He uses this method principally with Julien and Mathilde, though there is an interesting example in Part II, chapter 34 where an interior monologue in the mind of the marquis is introduced in order to guide the reader towards a better understanding of Julien, without any overt authorial statement.

Stendhal's ideas about style were the result of years of reflection on literary fashions in France throughout the early decades of the nineteenth century. A theme recurring frequently in his notes on style is the importance of precision of meaning and of vigour. The episode of the courtship of Mme de Fervaques is used by Stendhal as a pretext for expressing some of his views on bad style, as when Julien is amused by the letters of Korasoff: ' "Est-il possible, se disait-il, qu'il se soit trouvé un jeune homme pour écrire ainsi!" Il compta plusieurs phrases de neuf lignes' (p.431). But it is precisely the length of the sentences which impresses the devout Mme de Fervaques, who reflects that it makes a desirable contrast with the sprightly style made fashionable by Voltaire, 'cet homme si immoral'. Her own letters commit the cardinal sin of imprecision of meaning: 'Le vague était complet. Cela voulait tout dire et ne rien dire. C'est la harpe éolienne du style, pensa Julien' (p.434). The aeolian harp, an instrument left to vibrate in the wind and not controlled by human hand, is an amusing Stendhalian metaphor for bad style. One of his models of good style was the eighteenth-century writer the Président de Brosses, and in his diary on May 1 1815 he wrote: 'Le style qui me plaît le plus est celui de de Brosses qui dit beaucoup et des choses très fortes, en peu de mots et très clairement, avec grâce, et sans pédanterie' (*3*, I, p.927). A relevant example of the sort of rhetoric detested by Stendhal can be found in the newspaper account of the Berthet trial. This article, included by P.-G. Castex in the appendix of his excellent edition of the novel (*2*), provides an instructive contrast to Stendhal's fictional version, which uses the central fact but strips it of cliché and facile dramatisation:

> Julien entra dans l'église neuve de Verrières. Toutes les fenêtres hautes de l'édifice étaient voilées avec des rideaux cramoisis. Julien se trouva à quelques pas derrière le banc de Mme de Rênal. Il lui sembla qu'elle priait avec ferveur. La vue de cette femme qui l'avait tant aimé fit trembler le bras de Julien d'une telle façon, qu'il ne put d'abord exécuter son dessein. Je ne le puis, se disait-il à lui-même; physiquement, je ne le puis.
>
> En ce moment, le jeune clerc qui servait la messe sonna pour l'*élévation*. Mme de Rênal baissa la tête qui un instant se trouva presque entièrement cachée par les plis de son châle. Julien ne la reconnaissait plus aussi bien; il tira sur elle un coup de pistolet et la manqua; il tira un second coup, elle tomba. (p.480)

This crucial episode is narrated with such economy of words and of explanations that it seems obscure. What is the significance of the crimson curtains? It is apparently an allusion to the events of Part I, chapter 5, when there was a premonition of the crime, but Stendhal provides no helpful reminder of the connection despite its possible importance. Why does Julien seem reluctant to shoot Mme de Rênal, and then do the deed? These questions are implicit in the text but the novelist provides no answers, preferring to give the episode a certain opacity. The element of uncertainty concerns the motivation of Julien. It is paradoxical that a writer who stressed his attachment to clarity should occasionally choose to mystify us in this way, and this was a feature of Stendhal which perplexed many of his contemporary readers. It is significant that even Flaubert was to declare that he could not understand the intentions of the author of *Le Rouge et le Noir*. It was to be Stendhal's good fortune that distant posterity would tend to see opacity as evidence of profundity, and as a quality which stimulates the imagination of the reader.

In fact Stendhal himself later came to the conclusion that his pursuit of narrative economy and concision had been carried too far. Taking that historical perspective which was so characteristic, he explained this as a reaction against the sometimes verbose and unsubtle style in the plays of Hugo and Dumas and in the successful novels of George Sand. Stendhal believed that their style would prevent their works from passing on to posterity. In a note written in 1834 on his own copy of *Le Rouge et le Noir* he commented: 'Dans quel style néologique et admiré G. Sand eût traduit tout ceci! Le roman est-il une composition essentiellement éphémère? Si vous voulez plaire infiniment aujourd'hui, il faut vous résoudre à être ridicule dans vingt ans. Depuis que la démocratie a peuplé les théâtres de gens grossiers, incapables de comprendre les choses fines, je regarde le Roman comme la Comédie du XIXe siècle' (2, p.494). This significant statement shows Stendhal's high ambition for the new novel of·his time, and his real perspicacity in the question of style. It is indeed his disciplined writing which has a quality more lasting than that of George Sand. Already in a note made in his diary in 1810, we see him adopt a similar historical perspective in a comment on *La Nouvelle Héloïse*. If only Rousseau had been less didactic, declared the young Stendhal, he could have been 'le Mozart de la langue française et aurait produit un bien plus grand effet que Mozart sur les cœurs des hommes. Mais il voulait en être le législateur et non les ravir' (3, p.974). There is no doubt that Stendhal's hope was to be this literary Mozart who would bring together gaiety and occasional melancholy, who would charm both our minds and our emotions.

3. A Portrait of a Society

Readers of *Le Rouge et le Noir* should not assume that its analysis of French society is a detached and objective one. Stendhal's novel is in reality a partisan fictional account by an individual who had his own political convictions. At times these opinions are expressed directly, but more often they are present in less obvious ways which are a challenge to the reader. The novel also contains an element of difficulty due to the fact that fiction inspired by political themes often seems obscure to posterity. This is a problem of which Stendhal was very aware and he discusses it openly in Part II, chapter 22, where there is an imaginary debate between author and publisher. The author expresses the fear that reference to the politics of 1830 will soon make the novel dated, will be like a discordant note in a work of fiction, and will offend those readers whose opinions are different. The fictional publisher retorts that these risks must be accepted because political issues are such a preoccupation of the French nation in 1830 that an author who claims to be holding up a mirror to contemporary France cannot omit them.

The historical setting is that of the Bourbon monarchy which, after a false start in 1814, established itself in 1815 with the help of foreign armies after the overthrow of Napoleon. It lasted only until 1830, and Stendhal, who wrote much of his novel in that very year, must have sensed that the unpopular regime was stumbling towards its destruction. Intended as a contribution to the propaganda war against it, *Le Rouge et le Noir* had the misfortune to be published in late 1830, a few months after the July Revolution had swept away Charles X and his government. Seen in historical perspective, Stendhal's novel deserves a lasting place in French literature as a fine example of polemical fiction.

A political situation familiar to the first generation of readers now needs explanation, as does the political bias of Stendhal's

novel, which was certainly more clear in 1830 than it is in our time.
The programme of the monarchy, restored to power after a quarter
of a century which saw the Revolution, the rise and fall of the
Republic and that of Napoleon, was to reverse as many as possible
of the social and political changes which had taken place during this
extraordinary era. The two main forces of reaction were the nobles
and the clergy, who hoped for a return of confiscated property and
lost power. They formed an alliance which was metaphorically
known as that of the throne and the altar. Their adversaries called
the extremists ultra-royalists, then the term was shortened to ultras.
Their symbolic colour was white, as in the traditional flag bearing
the fleur de lys, and that of the clergy was the black of clerical garb.
The significance of the colours in Stendhal's title has caused much
discussion, and Roger Pearson (*34*) has provided an interesting
summary of the conflicting theories, some of them fanciful. It is
worth noting that even the contemporaries of Stendhal were
uncertain about the title, a fact which again underlines the
enigmatic tendency which is a feature of his writing. It seems
reasonable to accept the comment made in 1842 by Stendhal's
friend Emile Forgues, who had also felt the need to ask the author
for an explanation. Forgues reported that he got the reply that the
colour red meant that if the ambitious Julien had been born earlier
he could have risen high in the army of the Empire, whereas the
new France of the Restoration left a man of his class with no career
option apart from the Church. When Julien is in the seminary, he
reflects: 'Sous Napoléon, j'eusse été sergent; parmi ces futurs curés,
je serai grand vicaire' (p.196). When he has momentary doubts
about a clerical career, it is made clear that he could still join the
army as an ordinary soldier, or become a teacher, but that this
would mean an end to any hope of self-betterment: 'Ce moment fut
le plus éprouvant de sa vie. Il lui était si facile de s'engager dans un
des beaux régiments en garnison à Besançon! Il pouvait se faire
maître de latin; il lui fallait si peu pour sa subsistance! Mais alors
plus de carrière, plus d'avenir pour son imagination: c'était mourir'
(p.205). One of the recurring thoughts in Julien's mind is a nostal-
gic admiration for the military adventures of the armies of

Napoleon, and despite the fact that the novelist neglects to provide any helpful explanation, the colour red had been a significant feature of the uniform of many imperial regiments, often being used for epaulettes and plumes. It was also the colour of the uniform of those who held high grades in the imperial War Ministry in which Stendhal worked as a young man, and of the *légion d'honneur* proudly worn by Julien's mentor the retired army surgeon. We can therefore conclude with some confidence that the red and the black are symbols of the differing careers open to an unprivileged youth before and after 1815.

Stendhal's portrayal of the political opposition to the royalist government shows the three major factions, namely the liberals, the republicans and the bonapartists. Bonapartist sentiment is represented mainly by Julien himself, though he chooses to hide it in order to further his rise in society. Napoleon had died in 1821 and Stendhal did not see bonapartism as a serious political option without the Emperor, but he clearly indicates its continuing appeal to an underprivileged section of society which associated it with social mobility. This can be seen in the conversation in which two masons discuss military service in the France of 1815-1830:

> — Hé bien y faut partir, v'là une nouvelle conscription.
> — Dans le temps *de l'autre*, à la bonne heure; un maçon y devenait officier, y devenait général, on a vu ça.
> — Va-t'en voir maintenant! il n'y a que les gueux qui partent. Celui qui a *de quoi* reste au pays.
> — Qui est né misérable, reste misérable, et v'là. (p.218)

Julien listens with approval to this conversation, in which the continuation of the Napoleonic legend is shown, with one of the workmen refusing to believe that the Emperor is dead. As for French republicanism, it receives only small representation in *Le Rouge et le Noir*, notably in the minor character Fouqué who is portrayed very sympathetically. Although the period 1815–30 was marked by a significant number of bonapartist and republican conspiracies and trials, Stendhal makes little mention of this aspect of contemporary history, preferring to concentrate on the satirical portrayal of his political adversaries. Among these are the liberals in the little town of Verrières who are shown as a coarse and greedy class of factory owners, bankers, and civil servants who are courted and manipulated by the royalist Valenod.

The real political venom in Stendhal's novel is directed at ambitious priests and at a secret association called the *congrégation*, the existence of which has been authenticated by historians. Its members were both clerics and laymen, and it was organised in the manner of the freemasons, with no distinction as to social class, and was controlled by the Jesuits. *Le Rouge et le Noir* contains frequent references to the *congrégation*, and attributes to it a power which is already considerable at the start of the action, when the virtuous priest Chélan is about to be replaced by the unscrupulous Maslon, and which has become even greater by the end. When the jealous M. de Rênal considers catching his wife in the arms of Julien and killing her, he reflects that the protection of the *congrégation* would preserve a royalist mayor from serious consequences. The episode of a fraudulent auction manipulated by Maslon in order to favour Saint-Giraud is part of the same political theme: 'Quelle infamie! disait un gros homme à la gauche de Julien (…). —Bah! lui répondait un jeune fabricant libéral, M. de Saint-Giraud n'est-il pas de la congrégation?' (p.168). The priests Castanède and Frilair are also active members, and it is principally in the role played by the latter that Stendhal makes his attack on the shadowy corporation. He gives Frilair immense power in Besançon, where he is 'cet homme adroit qui avait organisé si savamment le réseau de la congrégation bisontine, et dont les dépêches à Paris faisaient trembler juges, préfet et jusqu'aux officiers généraux de la garnison' (p.219). Later in the action the ambitious priest has confirmed his power in Paris, where he can manipulate the functioning of the legal system, for example being secretly in league with six of the jurymen in the trial of Julien (p.510). The fact that Julien is condemned to death in spite of Frilair is due to the influence of Valenod, another member of the *congrégation*, who uses the rigged jury in an act of personal vengeance. As a fictional portrayal of the growing power of a secret and tentacular organisation led by unscrupulous individuals, *Le Rouge et le Noir* makes a dramatic accusation about the social role of the Catholic Church. An important part of this theme is the episode set in the Besançon seminary, which is depicted as an establishment where blind obedience and conformity are encouraged. The future priests do not value learning, preferring to think of their next meal and of the good living they will have in their future parish. Spying and denunciation are rife in the seminary, where Castanède is extending the influence of the *congrégation* among the next generation of priests. The negative portrayal of the seminary is balanced to some extent by the presence of some good priests like the honest Pirard, and by the novelist's comment on the attraction of the clerical career. Julien's initial scorn for the ignorant sons of farmers is tempered by pity when he reflects that they had known poverty, and saw priesthood as an escape from hunger. Their vocation was not to religion, but to warm clothes and regular meals. In this way Stendhal, though he paints a disturbing picture, also shows understanding and gives a social explanation of the abuses he is denouncing.

Should the reader see Stendhal's anti-clerical satire as a gross exaggeration? Although it is not possible either to prove or to disprove the total historical accuracy of figures like Castanède, one can be sure that the novelist allowed himself that element of deliberate enhancement of reality which is so much a part of political fiction. It is however true that the royalist and Catholic discourse of the time was itself close to self-caricature, as can be seen even today if one studies the relevant newspapers. Modern historians have thrown light on the manner of Stendhal's use of a contemporary event which inspired one episode in his novel. This was a religious ceremony celebrated with pomp in Paris in 1830, and involving the bones of St Vincent de Paul. The ceremony was led by the archbishop of Paris, eager to encourage the old custom of the veneration of relics as an antidote to modern scepticism. The handsome and aristocratic prelate, known for the grace of his benedictions, certainly provided the inspiration for Stendhal's Bishop of

Agde. It is equally clear that Stendhal's fictional monarch at the shrine of St Clement was inspired by the pious Charles X, and the allusion would have been clear to many readers. Just below the surface of the text lies a contemporary reality which the novelist has modified for his needs, and some of his first readers could also have named real individuals who resemble Mme de Fervaques, Altamira and other minor characters. But the enduring quality of Stendhal's novel is linked to its fictional nature, in which social realities have made their contribution to a narrative which is autonomous. The political facts are present under the fiction, adapted and transformed by the imagination of the novelist, like a foundation which is obscured by an edifice but essential to it.

Another major theme in *Le Rouge et le Noir* is that of French provincial life, which Stendhal believed to be an identifiable cultural phenomenon. His study of it takes up much of the first half of the novel, the second part being mostly devoted to a contrasting study of Parisian character and behaviour. A provincial himself, but one who had lived for many years in Paris and in Italy, his portrait of French country character is an analysis of a reality from which he had fled. The theme is introduced early with M. de Rênal, whose position as mayor of the town of Verrières gives him a symbolic role as a representative of small-town characteristics. The reader first sees the mayor through the eyes of an imaginary visitor from Paris, and this observer starts with a good impression which is soon modified when he sees in M. de Rênal 'un certain air de contentement de soi et de suffisance mêlé à je ne sais quoi de borné et de peu inventif' (p.14). To this accusation of self-satisfaction and lack of imagination is added one of avarice, shown both in M. de Rênal and in old Sorel. In addition, these Stendhalian provincials have the serious defect of being opposed to new aesthetic ideas such as the Italian style of architecture which is influencing Paris. In M. de Rênal, Stendhal mocks a country conservatism which he declares to be intolerable for anyone who has known the freedom of life in the capital. His novel is the account of the self-liberation of two privileged provincials, Julien Sorel and Mme de Rênal.

Stendhal's severe comments on the inhabitants of Verrières

often have the appearance of an act of personal vengeance on his own home town, but the matter is a complex one because his theory of provincial character also attributes to it some of the finest human qualities. The timber-merchant Fouqué is a personification of loyalty and generosity, and his offer to sell his property to save his friend brings an explicit statement from a grateful Julien that his character is sublime, and he asks 'quel est celui de ces beaux Parisiens qui serait capable d'un tel sacrifice?' (p.490). And the character of Julien is an assertion of a similar provincial superiority of energy and ambition. The theme is strongly expressed in the episode where he crosses the mountain to visit Fouqué (p.87). As Julien's ardent imagination looks forward to a life in Paris full of great deeds and the love of a superior woman, the author intervenes to state that no young Parisian would have the confident, striving energy of this country youth. In Stendhal's system of values the provincial element in the character of Julien is of central importance, and almost equal to that of class. The other major incarnation of the theory of rural superiority is Mme de Rênal, to whom Julien returns late in the action, rejecting the Parisian Mathilde. Mme de Rênal is portrayed as an ideal figure, and her superior nature is linked to the environment. We can conclude that Stendhal portrayed provincial France as being capable of producing the worst and the best in humanity, both the rapacity of Valenod and that ideal simplicity and generosity which he personified in Mme de Rênal. His Parisian characters illustrate his belief that the cultural milieu of the capital formed individuals with more refinement but lacking that energy which was a source of fascination to him.

A social theme of lasting interest in *Le Rouge et le Noir* is that of the position of women in society, a subject already traditional in the serious French novel, and the situation of Mme de Rênal is an explicit comment on marriage in France. Mme de Rênal is portrayed as a woman who is happy as a mother, and who is at first not actively dissatisfied as a wife. She believes the insensitivity of her husband and his love of money and status to be a universal male characteristic, and Stendhal adopts her viewpoint to make his most sweeping condemnation of French provincial men: 'La grossièreté, et la plus brutale insensibilité à tout ce qui n'était pas intérêt d'argent, de préséance ou de croix; la haine aveugle pour tout raisonnement qui les contrariait, lui parurent des choses naturelles à ce sexe, comme porter des bottes et un chapeau de feutre' (p.50). It is only after contact with Julien that Mme de Rênal becomes dissatisfied, and from this point the novelist gives general social significance to her role as a person whose marital infidelity, because she is a woman, could lead to her being banished from her children and from her home, and to a ruined life. Enlisting the sympathy of the reader for the adulterous heroine with a vigour not found in the novels of the Restoration, Stendhal endows her with energy and imagination as she acts to counter an anonymous letter sent to her husband. The attitude of the novelist is clearly seen in the implicit criticism of the angry words of M. de Rênal: 'Quel bon sens peut-on espérer d'une femme? Jamais vous ne prêterez attention à ce qui est raisonnable; comment sauriez-vous quelque chose? Votre nonchalance, votre paresse ne vous donnent d'activité que pour la chasse aux papillons, êtres faibles et que nous sommes malheureux d'avoir dans nos familles' (p.146). The story of Mme de Rênal is intended as an argument against the custom of arranged marriages, still common at the time. The bond which forms between her and her young lover is presented not only as a touching story of love between a man and a woman, but also as the basis of an ideal family unit, natural not social, because it is founded on sentiment, and M. de Rênal's affection for his sons is less than that of Julien. This Stendhalian critique of formal marriage is also expressed in the episode of Mathilde's love-affair with Julien, where the novelist describes her response to the prospect of marriage with M. de Croisenois, and a life full of ease but devoid of emotion. It is no accident that *Le Rouge et le Noir* contains two heroines who bear a feminist message about the situation of women in society.

The dominant theme in Stendhal's portrayal of contemporary society is that of class. As we have seen in the first chapter, it was unusual for a serious French novelist of this time to have a protagonist who was not an aristocrat, and this remains a lasting part of the interest of Stendhal's novel. Julien's career begins as a manual worker in his father's saw-mill, and he lives in a state of poverty and dependence because of the avarice of old Sorel. But Julien's story is essentially one of social mobility and of employment of a different sort, firstly as tutor, then as private secretary. Already by the time of entry into the seminary Julien feels personally distanced from the unrefined sons of farmers around him, just as he had felt different from his own family and from his friend Fouqué, who is from the same provincial class as the Sorel family.

Much of Part I is devoted to the portrayal of the class represented by M. de Rênal, namely the minor provincial nobility whose social and political situation had improved considerably with the return of the monarchy. This is why the novelist comments in the opening chapter that, since 1815, M. de Rênal is embarrassed at being a factory-owner instead of living solely from his property in the traditional aristocratic manner. A recurrent theme in Part I is the obsessive feeling of social inferiority of Julien towards the family of M. de Rênal. This is repeatedly made clear, as when Julien thinks resentfully of them as 'ces nobles si fiers' (p.93), and the fact is important because the class to which Stendhal gives most prominence is the nobility. The most significant distinction in *Le Rouge et le Noir* is not between worker and bourgeois, a difference which can be defined in economic terms, but the greater social chasm between aristocrat and commoner.

As portrayed by Stendhal, the French aristocracy is obsessed by the fear of a recurrence of the massacres of 1793. The memory of the Revolution is frequently present, as in the authorial comment on Julien's angry reaction to criticism by M. de Rênal: 'Ce sont sans doute de tels moments d'humiliation qui ont fait les Robespierre' (p.70). A similar connection is made between Julien and the men of the Revolution when Mathilde hears him expressing admiration for Danton, and feels afraid of him. Mme de Rênal speaks more than once of the same fear of renewed class war: 'S'il y a une nouvelle révolution, tous les nobles seront égorgés' (p.174). Portraying the nobility as being fearful and defensive, Stendhal condemns it as a class which is unsure of itself, negative and backward-looking.

The novelist's most memorable picture of the French aristocracy is in Part II with the portrayal of the ultra-conservative social
circle of M. de La Mole. The marquis has a nostalgia for absolute
monarchy and rejects modern fashion by wearing a wig, a detail
which carries a symbolic message, as does the extremely small head
of his son Norbert. Owing to the sense of propriety of Mme de La
Mole and the antipathy of the marquis for new ideas, the subjects of
conversation are severely limited. Consequently, the members of the
aristocratic salon suffer from chronic boredom and from an
'asphyxie morale' so pervasive that few would attend were it not for
the political power of M. de La Mole (p.274). He has excellent
connections at Court which he uses without scruple in order to
extend his influence, being quite prepared to have Valenod
nominated to high office in return for his allegiance and in spite of
his lack of principle. The marquis also has inside knowledge of
government decisions which he uses in the stock exchange in order
to increase his already large fortune. His house resembles a royal
court with its inner circle formed by members of the old aristocracy
and by a group of ambitious individuals who pay homage in the
hope of eventual reward. The noble family looks with scorn on
commoners and on those of recent title. M. de Croisenois, Norbert
de La Mole and M. de Caylus enjoy ridiculing those less fashionable
than themselves. Julien speaks for the author when he draws the
conclusion that behind this idle denigration lies a hidden envy of
those whose lives are less privileged but more active.

It should be noted that Stendhal's portrayal of the aristocracy
is not a simple condemnation. Although Julien is bitterly aware of
their tendency to scorn him as a commoner, he is also charmed by
them, as already observed. This is the case in his relations with
Norbert de La Mole and with the marquis, and is particularly clear
in the episode of M. de Beauvoisis and in that of Korasoff. Julien
admires the grace and wit of M. de Beauvoisis and his friends, who
have none of the prudish hypocrisy of the salon of Mme de La Mole:
'L'ennui n'est donc point inhérent, se disait-il, à une conversation
entre gens de haute naissance!' (p.292). The attractive nature of
aristocratic manners is also strongly expressed in the character of

Korasoff, the Russian prince who befriends Julien and impresses him with his generosity and ability to enjoy life. The portrayal of the aristocracy in these minor figures shows the complexity of the attitude of Stendhal, who questions the privileges enjoyed by the nobility but admires a certain aristocratic ethos.

Stendhal's main political statement about the aristocracy is made through the marquis de la Mole and his daughter Mathilde, and an important part of it is in the episode of the Secret Note. Although this part of the novel would have been easy for most of Stendhal's contemporaries to understand, this is certainly not the case for the majority of modern readers who do not know the details of the political situation in 1830. The marquis asks Julien to take a secret message from a group of aristocratic plotters to the representative of a foreign power. As high treason is involved, it is deemed safer not to put the Note in writing but to get Julien to learn it by heart. He attends the meeting of the conspirators and at once realises that a conservative revolution to overthrow the constitution is being planned. The most eloquent spokesman of the plotters is the marquis, who calls for a pre-emptive coup to destroy the parliamentary system. His plan is that the aristocracy will seize power by creating an armed militia of loyal peasants who are not contaminated by new ideas. A reactionary regime is then to be consolidated by an intervention of foreign monarchies hostile to a political system which they fear may spread in Europe. The marquis calls on his colleagues to prepare for a class war in which their survival is at stake: 'Entre la liberté de la presse et notre existence comme gentilhommes il y a guerre à mort. Devenez des manufacturiers, des paysans, ou prenez votre fusil' (p.405). The most fanatical members of the plot include a bishop, a cardinal and the prime minister. When Julien is on his way to the frontier there is an attempt to intercept him, led by the sinister Jesuit Castanède, whose clerical masters are hostile to a conspiracy which they do not control. Julien succeeds in meeting the foreign prince, to whom he communicates the request for military support for the planned royalist coup, and returns to France with a reply which disappoints M. de La Mole.

The episode of the Secret Note raises some questions which I

shall try to answer. Why does the novelist show the marquis entrust-
ing a mission of such significance to Julien, who is not a natural
ally, and whose subversive political opinions must be partly known
to him? This does not appear to be fully logical. Do the detailed
physical descriptions of some conspirators mean that Stendhal
expected readers to be able to decode the text and provide the names
of actual individuals in fictional disguise? Who is this tall, thin man
with several waistcoats? Was this portrayal of royalists plotting to
overthrow the constitution historically accurate? Was the novelist in
danger of prison because of his inclusion in the conspiracy of a
prime minister, the fictional M. de Nerval? Or was the episode
written and safely added only as an afterthought, in the period
between the Revolution of 1830 and the actual appearance of the
novel a few months later?

All the evidence suggests that the politically sensitive episode
of the Secret Note was incorporated in the novel months before the
Revolution of 1830 swept away the regime portrayed by Stendhal.
The secret mission is mentioned early in part II, and several other
references show it to be fully integrated into the action. Although
one cannot assert that Stendhal's accusation of royalist conspiracy
was made without risk, it was unlikely that there would be serious
consequences for himself, because the censors considered novels
unworthy of consideration and concentrated on plays, newspapers
and even on satirical poems. Moreover, the accusation of royalist
conspiracy had already been made openly in the opposition press, as
H.-F. Imbert has shown (28). The episode of conspiracy in *Le Rouge
et le Noir* is a fictional version of these charges, and Stendhal's
novel was therefore a calculated contribution to the campaign
against the regime of Charles X. As for historical accuracy,
Stendhal's picture of a fanatical prime minister plotting to
overthrow the constitution certainly did not seem very far from
reality to contemporary readers who knew something about
Polignac, the actual holder of the office. Although it is clear that
Stendhal's portrayal of his political adversaries shows some
deliberate distortion, he was aware of the fact that propaganda is
effective only if it contains significant elements of truth, and he used

these as a springboard for his imagination. The episode of the Secret Note is an act of disinformation, but one which is prophetic and contains some historical realities. Unfortunately, its literary quality is not equal to its political interest, and it must be said that the great European drama of the struggle between monarchies and nations deserved a more lucid and disciplined form. One of Stendhal's main ideas in this polemical portrayal of the political ambitions of the aristocracy is not made sufficiently clear, namely the use of Julien, a potential class enemy, as secret agent of the royalists. By making the marquis have recourse to Julien in preference to his own son or his friends, the novelist introduces a factor of symbolic significance: the alleged inability of the aristocracy to produce men of sufficient ability to ensure its hold on power.

The relationship between Mathilde and Julien makes a similar symbolic statement about the classes which they represent. With her beauty and regal manners, Mathilde personifies an aristocratic ideal. She is admired by all at the ball of the Duc de Retz where the men of fashion speculate that she could hope for the hand of some sovereign prince. But Mathilde is unhappy at the thought of a fashionable life, and has no enthusiasm for the distinguished young men around her: 'Quoi de plus plat, se dit-elle, que tout ce groupe! Voilà Croisenois qui prétend m'épouser; il est doux, poli, il a des manières parfaites comme M. de Rouvray. Sans l'ennui qu'ils donnent, ces messieurs seraient fort aimables' (p.307). In a witty paradox, she reaches the conclusion that the only real social distinction is not good manners or a civil honour, but a death sentence, as it denotes individuality and energy. It is Altamira, a political refugee condemned to death in his own country, who inspires this conclusion which is a prefiguration of her relationship with Julien. Like the rest of her class, Mathilde often thinks of the Revolution of 1789, and fears a recurrence. When Julien in a moment of angry indiscretion reveals his admiration for Danton, Mathilde sees him as a potential enemy and her first reaction is one of fear.

The subsequent evolution of Mathilde constitutes one of the most original themes in *Le Rouge et le Noir*, as she comes to the conclusion that a revolution is likely to happen, and that she would prefer to be on the same side as Julien. Her readiness to break with her class is reasoned and explicit:

> Bien loin de redouter sans cesse une révolution comme mes cousines, qui, de peur du peuple, n'osent pas gronder un postillon qui les mène mal, je serai sûre de jouer un rôle, car l'homme que j'ai choisi a du caractère et une ambition sans bornes. (p.377)

Confirmation of the significance of Mathilde's choice is given in the letter telling her father that she is pregnant and about to marry the commoner Julien. All social links between them are broken, she declares, and again the theme of Julien as revolutionary is stressed: 'S'il y a révolution, je suis sûre pour lui d'un premier rôle. Pourriez-vous en dire autant d'aucun de ceux qui ont demandé ma main?' (p.460). In Mathilde, proud aristocrat of superior intelligence who rejects her own social group in favour of an energetic class enemy, Stendhal has made a statement about the decadence of the aristocracy. The fact that Julien is later given a title because of the influence of the marquis, and is magically transformed into M. le chevalier de La Vernaye, is part of a satirical portrayal of social elevation and of aristocratic distinction. Created with a mixture of irony and admiration, highly charged with political significance, Mathilde and the marquis are two of Stendhal's most interesting characters. They were to prove to be among the last major fictional portrayals of the aristocracy in the French novel, soon to be dominated by characters representing the middle class.

4. Psychology

One of Stendhal's most striking comments on fictional characters was made in an article on *Le Rouge et le Noir* written by himself in 1832, and included in the Castex edition (2). A great and growing number of novels were sold and read in the France of his time, especially by women, he said. These books were divided into two categories, according to the cultural level of the readers, and were informally known in the trade as novels for chambermaids and novels for ladies. The main characteristic of the former, which were widely read in the provinces and not only by chambermaids, was the idealised nature of the heroine and of the hero, always a perfect gentleman and extremely handsome. He explains that his intention was to produce a work which avoided the clichés of this sort of popular and sentimental novel in order to be read by discerning Parisian ladies: 'Rien ne semble plus fade, à Paris, que ce héros toujours parfait, que ces femmes malheureuses, innocentes et persécutées, des romans de femmes de chambre' (2, p.714). In fact Julien Sorel and Mathilde de La Mole are so far from the literary models of the time that they caused reactions of surprise and of incomprehension among many readers.

The unconventional portrayal of Julien begins with the outline of his family situation. Already in his first appearance he is shown as an anomalous individual, disliked by his father and brothers, different from them, and hating them. Angry because his son is reading a book instead of supervising a mechanical saw, old Sorel gives him a blow which almost precipitates him into the works of the machine. In this way the novelist uses an act of hostility as a symbol for the relations between Julien and his family. There is no mention of a mother, a fact which has significance in the light of Julien's future connection with Mme de Rênal, which clearly has an Oedipal dimension, as does his hostile relationship with his father.

There is a suggestion that Julien, who is physically different from his brothers, may not really be the son of old Sorel, but of the retired army surgeon who lodges with the family. This character acts as a substitute father to Julien, as do Pirard and M. de La Mole later in the action, providing an emotional compensation for the absence of affection and support from Sorel, whose status is reduced to that of presumed biological father. The novelist also provides another form of compensation for the deprived childhood of his hero, alone in a hostile male family, namely the power to charm women. This can be detected in the attitude of the village girls, then in the attraction of Elisa, of Mme de Rênal, of Amanda Binet, of Mathilde, of Mme de Fervaques and finally in the sentiments of ladies who cry at Julien's trial. But the first description of Julien stresses negative and destructive emotions, his anger and hatred of his father, and his 'air méchant'. All of this certainly places Julien a long way from the gentleman hero of the popular and sentimental novel. The character is drawn not so much from literary models as from the traumas, obsessions and fantasies of Stendhal's own troubled childhood, and it is this fact which gives it psychological coherence and power.

The development of the character of Julien is divided into three main phases marked by his relationships with Mme de Rênal, with Mathilde, and finally with Mme de Rênal again. The personality of Julien is the consequence of a combination of external factors (history, family, cultural influence) with intrinsic characteristics (energy, pride, ambition). His ambition is inspired largely by the example of Napoleon, whose name recurs frequently. The young Bonaparte, who won the heart of his social superior Mme de Beauharnais and rose to high position by means of the military profession, provides a role-model for Julien. When he turns to a career in the Church, he must hide his admiration of the fallen Emperor, but it remains concentrated inside him and is liable to betray itself in passionate outbursts which are dangerous for a student of theology in the France of Charles X. These lapses from his plan of conduct cause him to engage in strange acts of self-punishment which are part of a strategy for the achievement of mastery over himself in order to be able to have power over others.

But it seems that some greater force may be secretly directing the life of Julien, as is hinted in the episode where he enters the village church in which he will one day commit the crime for which he will be executed. Before him he sees a piece of printed paper which is a sinister omen:

> Sur le prie-Dieu, Julien remarqua un morceau de papier imprimé, étalé là comme pour être lu. Il y porta les yeux et vit:
>
> *Détails de l'exécution et des derniers moments de Louis Jenrel, exécuté à Besançon, le…*
>
> Le papier était déchiré. Au revers on lisait les deux premiers mots d'une ligne, c'étaient: *Le premier pas.*
>
> "Qui a pu mettre ce papier là? dit Julien. Pauvre malheureux, ajouta-t-il avec un soupir, son nom finit comme le mien…" et il froissa le papier.
>
> En sortant, Julien crut voir du sang près du bénitier, c'était de l'eau bénite qu'on avait répandue: le reflet des rideaux rouges qui couvraient les fenêtres la faisaient paraître du sang. (p.37)

This episode is a detailed premonition of major events in the future life of Julien. His approaching the house where he will meet Mme de Rênal is the *first step*, the illusion of blood on the church floor anticipates the shooting of Mme de Rênal, and the name of Louis Jenrel who died on the guillotine is a perfect anagram for that of Julien Sorel. As is often the case in the literature of premonitions, the individual most concerned has an imperfect understanding of the omen, and so it is that Julien notices only that Jenrel ends like Sorel. Julien asks himself who could have put the paper there, and the novelist seems to suggest that it was the force of Destiny. This bears the extraordinary implication that the energy and independence of Julien are no more than illusion, and that his life can be seen as the blind fulfilment of acts dictated by some unknown force greater than individual will and intelligence.

However, the text is highly enigmatic in this important aspect of the novel, because the energy and apparent freedom of Julien seem central to the action. If Stendhal wished readers to see the life of Julien as a negation of personal liberty and free-will, he certainly did not develop this theme in an explicit manner. On the contrary, the novelist seems to concentrate on the independence and upward striving of a superior individual. There is no authorial irony at the end of chapter 10 of Part I when he symbolically places Julien in a high and solitary position in a manner traditional for Romantic heroes. In the sky above him he sees the flight of a hawk as a sign of the power and elevation which he associates with Napoleon, and a few pages later the image of the bird of prey recurs insistently in an episode which again stresses the side of Julien which is solitary and suspicious of human society:

> Caché comme un oiseau de proie, au milieu des roches nues qui couronnent la grande montagne, il pouvait apercevoir de bien loin tout homme qui se serait approché de lui. Il découvrit une petite grotte au milieu de la pente presque verticale d'un des rochers. Il prit sa course, et bientôt fut établi dans cette retraite. "Ici, dit-il avec des yeux brillants de joie, les hommes ne sauraient me faire de mal." (p.86)

In Julien's sense of personal superiority, alienation and suffering pride, Stendhal has created a character of much complexity which includes a pathological and misanthropic tendency similar to what one sees in some other great Romantic figures such as René and Corinne. And Julien's distrust of humanity is equalled by humanity's distrust of Julien. This is expressed most clearly by Pirard, in his capacity as director of the seminary: 'Je vois en toi quelque chose qui offense le vulgaire. La jalousie et la calomnie te poursuivront' (p.216). The friendly priest draws the conclusion that God had given Julien 'cette nécessité d'être haï' in order to punish him for his pride. The events surrounding Julien's ending seem to give force to this analysis. It implies that the Fate which governs his life can be seen as a psychological destiny, an innate compulsion which drives an unusual individual to achievement or disaster.

Julien's awareness of exceptional ability is accompanied by a belief that his progress must be rapid, that his vital force cannot await events. He refuses the offer of temporary partnership with Fouqué because this mediocre existence could extinguish in him 'le feu sacré avec lequel on se fait un nom' (p.88) and deprive him of 'cette énergie sublime qui fait faire les choses extraordinaires' (p.89). In this cult of energy Napoleon provides a model, and the young Julien reads his writings with religious fervour. From him he learns to view life as a military campaign, and it is because of the Napoleonic influence that Julien starts the fateful courtship of Mme de Rênal. The episode in which Julien for the first time takes her hand reveals a psychological mechanism of importance for the understanding of his character. Napoleon's vision of a man's life as a duty to conquer, and of women as objects worthy of conquest, is what motivates Julien to try to hold the hand of his employer's wife. He does this from a sense of *devoir* which is not related to a moral good, but simply duty to himself as achiever and conqueror. He observes Mme de Rênal 'comme un ennemi avec lequel il va falloir se battre' (p.66) and prepares for the taking of her hand by reading Napoleon in order to strengthen his resolve. Like a soldier before an assault he is relieved that the darkness will lessen the danger, but he needs all his self-control in order to carry out his plan. When the parody of conquest is completed, Julien returns to the *Mémorial* in order to draw more moral power from it: 'Il avait fait *son devoir, et un devoir héroïque*. Rempli de bonheur par ce sentiment, il s'enferma à clef dans sa chambre, et se livra avec un plaisir tout nouveau à la lecture des exploits de son héros' (p.69). Stendhal's irony towards his young protagonist is nowhere stronger than in this episode.

The same irony is present in the scene in which Julien and Mme de Rênal become lovers. Again, Julien is dominated by a sense of duty, and by the model of masterful behaviour which he is copying. At this point there is an authorial statement about the consequences of Julien's psychological state, explaining that this imitation of an ideal model, which is part of what makes him a superior individual, is also what prevents him from achieving the happiness within his reach. This intrinsic tension between ambition and happiness is a major theme in *Le Rouge et le Noir*. Repressed by mistrust, pride and ambition, there is a hidden part of Julien which becomes visible at certain times. One of these instances is the first period of friendship with Mme de Rênal and her children during summer days at the country house in Vergy (p.64). The setting of steep mountains covered by oak woods provides a haven of natural beauty which creates emotional security in Julien, briefly freed from the constraints of a life of obedience and hypocrisy in the home of his employer. Such moments of instinctive happiness are not yet valued by the protagonist, who continues to apply himself to a role of calculation and self-discipline.

But there are indications of the existence of another Julien, half visible inside the imitator of Napoleon. In the cathedral of Besançon he is deeply moved by a religious ceremony and by the sound of the great bells, and there is an authorial explanation stating that a man capable of such exalted emotion and intense imagination was not suited to a life of self-advancement, but had a different vocation: 'Jamais il ne fera ni un bon prêtre, ni un grand administrateur. Les âmes qui s'émeuvent ainsi sont bonnes tout au plus à produire un artiste' (p.212). Stendhal, here speaking openly as master of his fictional world and controller of the destiny of Julien, gives a strong hint of future events. But the apprenticeship of Julien is not yet completed, as he has not freed himself from an ethic based on pride and personal ambition.

The second great phase in the emotional progress of Julien is his relationship with Mathilde, a fictional character as complex and original as the protagonist. Stendhal's intention to create in Mathilde a figure free from the convention of idealised heroines is clear from her first appearance. We are told of her beautiful eyes, which is consistent with tradition, but with the additional information that they show 'une grande froideur d'âme' (p.265). And at the second meeting Julien sees in Mathilde an 'air dur, hautain, et presque masculin'. What gradually emerges, without explicit indication by the author, is the psychological similarity of

Mathilde and Julien. An important part of this resemblance is their pride, and it is this characteristic which first causes Mathilde to respect Julien. When she overhears him revealing to Pirard that he has a low opinion of the aristocratic salon of Mme de La Mole, she thinks: 'Celui-là n'est pas né à genoux (...) comme ce vieil abbé' (p.275). She also resembles Julien in the superiority of her mind and in her desire for knowledge, and it is significant that they regularly meet in her father's library, of which they are the only users.

A striking characteristic of Mathilde, also shared with Julien, is high aspiration and dissatisfaction with everyday reality. Whereas the ambition of Julien is directed at social success, that of Mathilde, who is already rich and privileged, is an aspiration to the happiness she reads about in books. The main source of her discontent is the mediocrity of the men of the modern Parisian aristocracy. Just as Julien admires Napoleon, Mathilde has an ideal model in Queen Marguerite de Navarre. She lived in dramatic times in the 16th century, and was passionately in love with Boniface de La Mole who was executed for treason. Mathilde admires above all the strength of character of Marguerite, who had the audacity to engage in a forbidden passion and the courage to obtain the severed head of Boniface and carry it away for secret burial as a last gesture of love.

The historical figure of Boniface played an important part in Stendhal's conception of Mathilde, as the fictional La Mole family is deemed to be descended from Boniface, but to have become degenerate and incapable of audacity and passion. Frustrated by the limitations of life in modern France, Mathilde has a nostalgia for the France of the Renaissance, and sees this period torn by civil war as a source of heroism and inspiration greater even than the time of Napoleon. The dramatic death of Boniface and Marguerite's strange act of devotion provide a model of energy and love. What modern woman would have the courage to touch the head of her executed lover, she asks Julien? Mathilde's impatience with her own time and her cult of Renaissance France are symptoms of a Romanticism which Stendhal portrays with a touch of irony, but with essential approval. His attitude to Mathilde is a complex one, as her character is at once an affectionate critique of Romanticism and an expression of it. This can be seen in the chapters where Julien and Mathilde are gradually united by a common aspiration to an existence more intense than the one which contemporary reality seems to offer.

Also prominent in the character of Mathilde, and naturally linked to her cult of Boniface and Marguerite, is a personal vitality which expresses itself partly in domination. Chapter XI of Part II, with the heading: 'L'empire d'une jeune fille!', describes those around her as the victims of a wit full of cruelty: 'Dès qu'on déplaisait à Mlle de La Mole, elle savait punir par une plaisanterie si mesurée, si bien choisie, si convenable en apparence, lancée si à propos, que la blessure croissait à chaque instant, plus on y réfléchissait' (p.329). She considers the men around her to be lacking in energy; they have perfect manners but are predictable and insipid. Mathilde's dominance and desire to punish are an expression of frustration. Then the pride and virility of Julien provide Mathilde with the challenge for which she has been waiting: loving a man who represents danger and from whom she is separated by the barrier of class.

Stendhal had claimed in his 1824 study *De l'amour* that there were a number of definable categories of love, and according to this classification the type of sentiment experienced by Mathilde is 'l'amour de tête'. In Stendhalian theory this superficial form of affection is a product of the mind alone, and in Mathilde the birth of love is inspired not by an emotion but by a thought: 'Une idée l'illumina tout à coup: "J'ai le bonheur d'aimer, se dit-elle un jour, avec un transport de joie incroyable. J'aime, j'aime c'est clair! A mon âge, une fille jeune, belle, spirituelle, où peut-elle trouver des sensations, si ce n'est dans l'amour?"' (p.331). Having arisen from an affinity of mind and from a process of logic, Mathilde's relationship with Julien continues in the same intellectual manner. Her model is great passion as shown in novels such as *Manon Lescaut* and *La Nouvelle Héloïse*, and she exults in the thought of the drama ahead as she imagines herself and Julien playing a major political role in a France again experiencing great events. Being of forceful and decisive character, she takes the initiative by making a declaration of love to Julien and by inviting him to her room at midnight. This is important for understanding Stendhal because it exonerates Julien from the possible accusation that he seduced Mathilde for social advantage. The decision is taken by Mathilde, it is she who seduces him. All of this is communicated with the approval of the author; for the first time Mathilde now lives intensely. She is motivated by that restless desire for happiness which is strong in the Stendhalian hero.

But the satirical element in the portrayal of Mathilde is never absent for long and is evident in the skilful comedy of her first night with Julien. Mathilde needs all her resolve in order to carry out her plan to give herself to him if he has the audacity to climb to her window with a ladder. She is living a fantasy of passionate love and, in another reversal of convention, she sees her virginity not as a state which she has a duty to protect, but as one she has a duty to abandon with resolution: 'Mlle de La Mole croyait remplir un devoir envers elle-même et envers son amant. "Le pauvre garçon, se disait-elle, a été d'une bravoure achevée, il doit être heureux, ou bien c'est moi qui manque de caractère"' (p.365). This cerebral and fragile affection, coloured by her pride and wish to dominate, forms the major psychological study in the second part of *Le Rouge et le Noir*.

The essence of this portrayal is again the similarity between Mathilde and Julien, that shared pride and energy which make their relationship a long and fluctuating conflict. The battle begins shortly after they have become lovers, when Mathilde experiences regret and anger. Julien's reaction to her scorn is to seize a sword with the intention of killing her, an act which reveals the violence latent in him. But the surprising Mathilde responds positively to the danger and is 'heureuse d'une sensation si nouvelle' (p.370). Their evolving relationship is constantly marked by tension, and Mathilde has contrasting phases of pride and dominance which alternate with phases of self-abasement so extreme that they enter the realm of masochism: 'Punis-moi de mon orgueil atroce (...) tu es mon maître, je suis ton esclave, il faut que je te demande pardon à genoux d'avoir voulu me révolter' (p.383). The key to Mathilde is the fact that she must dominate or be dominated, being unable to achieve a serene and equal relationship with her lover. This is what Julien discovers when Korasoff provides a strategy of reconquest by arousing her jealousy. It is by application of this plan that Julien frees himself from her dominance by using her pride as a means to subjugate her, as she cannot bear his apparent indifference. Thus Mathilde comes to experience the maximum amount of emotion possible for a Parisian lady in disappointing modern times.

This portrayal of emotion complicated and falsified by calculation is a pessimistic vision of the psyche. The love experienced by Julien and by Mathilde produces two types of conflict. The first is that which exists between two persons, and which finds natural metaphorical expression in the military terms which recur in the mind of Julien in the early days of the relationship: 'Dans la bataille qui se prépare (…) l'orgueil de la naissance sera comme une colline élevée, formant position militaire entre elle et moi. C'est là-dessus qu'il faut manœuvrer' (p.352). The second sort of conflict is that which is taking place within the mind of each lover, as when Mathilde alternates between rejection of Julien and submission to him. It is Julien especially who is reduced to self-hatred by his love, when he speaks of: 'cet être si odieux, que j'appelle *moi*' (p.431) and asks:'Pourquoi suis-je moi?' (p.441). In this manner, love is shown as a potential source of disintegration of the personality, the instinctive part of which is seen to be in destructive conflict with the part which thinks. Thus Julien resists 'la partie tendre' (p.458) of his nature in order to control both his own emotions and those of Mathilde, who must be dominated so that she does not dominate. The Stendhalian *amour de tête* brings only a limited form of happiness, and this is all that the novelist ever accords to Mathilde. She does not follow Julien in his eventual transformation, being ruled always by her pride, her awareness of others, her image of herself and by her overblown imagination.

Stendhal's attitude to Mathilde alternates so frequently between approval and satire that it is difficult to avoid speaking of ambiguity. It is clear that he admires her aspiration to happiness, her wish to live intensely, and her frustration in her life of easy privilege. Although she is capable only of phases of enthusiasm and passion, this is nevertheless an expression of her superiority over most women of Paris who, like Mme de Fervaques, suffer from 'l'impossiblité d'aucune vive émotion' (p.429). Similarly, Mathilde's superiority is asserted in her scorn for money, fine horses and châteaux, unlike other young women of the aristocracy. In her daring pursuit of what she wants, she is a free spirit. One of the most positive portrayals of Mathilde is in the episode in which she achieves for Julien a startling social promotion, including a gift of property, permission to marry her, an aristocratic title, and a commission in the army. Announcing her pregnancy to her father, Mathilde takes charge of the situation and acts with skill and determination. She is ready to abandon her social position, and courageously accepts responsibility: 'Je redoute pour Julien votre colère, si juste en apparence. Je ne serai pas duchesse, mon père; mais je le savais en l'aimant; car c'est moi qui l'ai aimé la première, c'est moi qui l'ai séduit' (p.459). After Julien's crime she continues to play a heroic role, resolutely attempting to save him. It therefore comes as a surprise when on the last page of the novel Stendhal censures her more severely than ever, again downgrading the strong, intelligent and courageous Mathilde to the level of a player of roles, to an eccentric imitation of Marguerite de Navarre. This final condemnation appears brusque and imperfectly integrated into the logic of the novel, exposing Stendhal to the charge that there is some incoherence in his attitude to the extraordinary and fascinating Mathilde.

The episode in which Stendhalian psychology can be seen in its most challenging form is that of the shooting of Mme de Rênal by Julien. This event is crucial because it ends Julien's rise in society and is followed by a profound change in his system of values. The first notable feature of Julien's act of violence is its reckless nature, being committed in public and during mass. The choice of a crowded church as a stage gives it a highly dramatic quality and adds the crime of sacrilege to that of attempted murder. What the reader must penetrate is the apparent enigma of Julien's motive and of his state of mind before the shooting of Mme de Rênal. Because of his recent social elevation, Julien's attachment to

Mathilde was at this time stronger than it had ever been. M. de La Mole, after his initial shock at the pregnancy of Mathilde, had come to accept the idea of Julien as son-in-law and member of his family. The bond of affection and esteem between them is about to be sanctioned formally. Learning the facts of the commencement of the love-affair and the essentially passive role of Julien, the marquis concedes: 'Ce n'est point là un méchant homme' (p.463). This favourable assessment of Julien is followed by a sacrificial act in which he gives the marquis a suicide note which would enable the wronged father to take vengeance. Julien's behaviour in this scene shows courage and a sense of honour. His provision of a suicide note is an impulsive act, but social instincts soon revive in Julien once they are given substance in the form of a gift of an estate from the marquis. In this episode the novelist adopts the viewpoint of M. de La Mole in order to make a statement about the character of the protagonist, in which he detects 'quelque chose d'effrayant' (p.471). The nature of this undefined element is still unclear, but the marquis is disturbed by it. This is confirmed in his letter of warning to Mathilde: 'Tremblez, jeune imprudente. Je ne sais pas encore ce que c'est que votre Julien, et vous-même vous le savez moins que moi' (p.473). M. de La Mole here speaks for Stendhal, as he brings his protagonist closer to the violent act in which the unknown becomes known and dramatically changes the course of the action.

When Julien has received from the marquis the gift of an estate, a title and a commission in the army, he has reached a high point in his career. His elevation is due to nepotism and is therefore not a real fulfilment of his youthful aspirations to military achievement, but Julien is dazzled by it and by his new aristocratic name, equally lacking in substance. At this point the novelist gives us, without comment, the thoughts of Julien: 'mon roman est fini, et à moi seul tout le mérite. J'ai su me faire aimer de ce monstre d'orgueil, ajoutait-il en regardant Mathilde; son père ne peut vivre sans elle, et elle sans moi' (p.474). Here the reader confidently detects implicit authorial disapproval of this cold, self-congratulating attitude now dominant in Julien, who exaggerates his own merit and undervalues that of Mathilde and her father. His artificial new social persona causes the imaginative Julien to indulge in fantasy about his real identity, as he actually begins to persuade himself of the credibility of his new incarnation as M. de La Vernaye. He surrenders to feelings of vanity, superiority and ambition, and his main preoccupation is now to become a general by the age of thirty. Intoxicated by social success, Julien is dominated by one side of his personality, as all emotions are subordinated to ambition. But coming events will redistribute the competing forces in his psyche and eventually reveal a different man.

The crisis in Julien's career of upward social mobility is caused by a letter in which Mme de Rênal accuses him of being a man who seduces women as a means to success. A rational and prudent policy for Julien would now be to play for time and to persuade the marquis that the accusation is untrue, which it certainly is. If that method failed there were other possibilities, such as Mathilde's earlier plan to start a new life with Julien in which he would begin as a teacher of Latin. But instead of trying to extricate himself from a situation which could still be saved, Julien commits an act of attempted murder which exposes him to the death penalty, and does so in front of numerous witnesses. His motives are never clearly explained by Stendhal, and have inspired critics to produce a number of theories, some more ingenious than convincing.

One alleged explanation of Julien's behaviour, in the time between reading the letter of accusation and the shooting of the woman who wrote it, is that the novelist implies that the protagonist was in a state of hallucination. According to this theory, Julien's inability to write a letter to Mathilde when travelling towards Verrières, and his difficulty in getting a gunsmith to understand that he wants to buy pistols, show that he is in a disturbed psychological state induced by rage. But these details can be more easily explained by the rapid movement of the carriage, which would make writing difficult, and by the comically talkative nature of the gunsmith, probably included by the novelist for reasons of contrast. Despite the suggestions made by some readers, the basic motivation of Julien is relatively simple, being one of vengeance. It should be noted that vengeance is not self-vindication, in fact being the exact opposite of this, as Julien does not seek to establish his innocence or merit, but deliberately commits a crime much worse than the misdemeanour of which he stands accused. Following the shooting, Julien explains in a letter to Mathilde that he acted in order to take revenge. This motive is confirmed in his own thoughts: 'J'ai été offensé d'une manière atroce; j'ai tué, je mérite la mort, mais voilà tout' (p.484). What is less easy to perceive is the precise state of mind of the protagonist at the time of the crime.

The solution to this mystery must be sought in the cryptic narration of his actions in the church of Verrières just before the shooting. We are told that Julien enters the building, notices the high windows covered by crimson curtains, and finds himself a little behind the pew of Mme de Rênal. He observes that she appears to be praying fervently. It is only now that the novelist gives us some real indication of the protagonist's state of mind: 'La vue de cette femme qui l'avait tant aimé fit trembler le bras de Julien d'une telle façon, qu'il ne put d'abord exécuter son dessein. Je ne le puis, se disait-il à lui-même; physiquement, je ne le puis' (p.480). It is only when Mme de Rênal lowers her head in prayer that he can bring himself to shoot her, because she is no longer so recognisable. It is therefore implied that Julien's crime is not an act of passion at the moment of action. His first reaction on reading the letter of denunciation had been one of rage and desire for vengeance. But when he is in the presence of Mme de Rênal there is inner conflict. The instinctive part of him responds to Mme de Rênal as a person, but the other part of his nature wins the battle and makes him follow an abstract principle of vengeance.

Once again Julien has imitated a theoretical model of behaviour, and once again he has used his steely will to force himself to carry out a course of action when it has been decided. Again it is Julien's artificial idea of duty to himself which has led him forward, and this time with disastrous consequences. Far from being unmotivated, Julien's crime expresses a part of his personality which has been coherently portrayed by the novelist. It is not so much inexplicable as unexplained, because Stendhal counts on the intuition and even the retentive memory of an ideal reader. He had already shown Julien's capacity for violence when he drew the sword on Mathilde, when he prepared to shoot Castanède and when he fired on the servants of Beauvoisis. Similar indications are the comment by the marquis on the unknown part of Julien, and Mathilde's hiding from him her father's letter of warning because: 'ce caractère farouche eût pu être porté à quelque folie' (p.474). The act of madness, the wild deed has now been done, and the destructive potential of Julien's character has become reality. That inability to tolerate scorn, that excessive pride which is such a dominant feature of his personality, allied to the determination which can lead to great achievement, has now brought Julien to an extremity. Stendhal has portrayed the admirable *folie* of an exceptional individual possessing the qualities which can lead either to great deeds or to disaster, and which he calls: 'le bonheur de se moquer de toute prudence, qui peut être si vif pour une âme ardente' (p.498). This Stendhalian ardour consumes the personality which harbours it as a flame consumes a candle. Julien's crime is a product of it, and may also be a consequence of an inscrutable Destiny which needs no logic but itself. But how many readers will remember the premonition given so early in the text in the brief mention of Louis Jenrel, whose name is an anagram of that of Julien Sorel and who precedes him to the guillotine? The paradox of Stendhalian psychology is that the protagonist is shown to be possibly ruled by Fate but also portrayed as a free agent, as a strong and autonomous individual who commits only the error of denying one part of his nature. Does the life of Julien show the irresistible force of Destiny? The enigmatic Stendhal asks the question but gives us no answer.

5. The Dénouement

Julien's crime and a gradual realisation of his error bring him to an evaluation of himself and to a different view of life, subjects which will dominate the episode following the catalytic event of his attack on Mme de Rênal. This dense and important section of the novel comprises ten chapters in which the narrative evolves in a new direction. At first there is a pause in the action, after the drama of the shooting in the church, and then the creation of suspense as the blade of the guillotine slowly rises over Julien. The main theme in the final episode is the personal development of the protagonist. His first statement to the examining magistrate is a declaration that he intended to kill with premeditation, a confession which he knows will make his crime into a capital offence. The self-destruction commenced in the church of Verrières is now being deliberately completed by what amounts to a legal suicide, a term which will later be used by M. de Frilair. An important fact for the understanding of the psychological state of Julien immediately after the shooting is the absence either of remorse or of any thought for his victim. He feels that he has been offended, has revenged himself, and is prepared to pay the penalty. His mind is full of abstractions such as honour, duty and vengeance, and the name of his victim does not once enter his thoughts at this time. Then there begins in Julien a change of crucial importance.

When the jailer brings the news that Mme de Rênal has survived, this precipitates in Julien one of those surges of emotion which he formerly sought to repress because he saw them as a form of self-revelation and vulnerability. The novelist now indicates more clearly one of the conflicting tendencies in the character of Julien, which he reveals only when he frees himself from curious eyes by ordering the jailer to leave the cell: 'Le géôlier obéit. A peine la porte fut-elle fermée: "Grand Dieu! elle n'est pas morte!" s'écria

Julien; et il tomba à genoux, pleurant à chaudes larmes' (p.485). In this moment of truth the invasion of Julien by emotion is so intense that it is accompanied by an unexpected religious impulse. Now Julien feels remorse for his crime, concern for Mme de Rênal, and a new serenity in accepting his coming punishment. The novelist stresses the voluntary nature of this acceptance by indicating the possibility of escape from the prison in Verrières and a new life in Switzerland, a chance which Julien rejects because of the thought of a long negotiation with the jailer. This serene and detached attitude to life and death is confirmed when he is taken to a new prison in Besançon. Here Julien looks on his surroundings with the eyes of an aesthete, and his place of incarceration is not some dark cell but high in an old tower of pleasing architecture and with a window which gives a magnificent view. This position of elevation and vision is symbolic, as once again he enjoys the pleasure earlier experienced by him in moments of isolation in high places, far from hostile eyes, free from ambition, from hypocrisy, from the need to act, and free to be himself. In a famous Stendhalian paradox, Julien's elevated prison with a view has become a metaphor for a happiness founded on lucidity and passive contemplation.

One of Julien's first realisations is the fact that he had already experienced real happiness, but had been blinded to the fact by his ambition for social success. He looks back at the days spent with Mme de Rênal in the country and now sees it as a lost paradise: 'Deux ou trois mille livres de rente pour vivre tranquille dans un pays de montagnes comme Vergy... J'étais heureux alors...Je ne connaissais pas mon bonheur!' (p.487). Thus Stendhal brings Julien to the assertion of a Romantic ideal in which happiness is linked to Nature and to an escape from a society which is portrayed in a manner increasingly negative. Julien rebuffs Mathilde and Fouqué when they relate their efforts to save him and says: 'Laissez-moi ma vie idéale. Vos petites tracasseries, vos détails de la vie réelle, plus ou moins froissants pour moi, me tireraient du ciel' (p.505). Aware of the unusual nature of his behaviour when faced by a probable death sentence, he underlines the paradox of the situation: 'Il est singulier pourtant que je n'aie connu l'art de jouir de la vie que depuis que j'en vois le terme si près de moi'. His discovery of the art of enjoying life now expresses itself through an explicit rejection of society.

The progressive condemnation of a society which is preparing to eliminate Julien marks the final episode of the novel. In an ironical depiction of the functioning of the system of trial by jury, the novelist shows M. de Frilair boasting to Mathilde that he can manipulate the court by giving instructions to a majority of the jurymen. They will vote not according to their conscience, but to save Julien as ordered by M. de Frilair's accomplice Valenod, who is chairman of the jury. The reward for M. de Frilair will be promotion to the rank of bishop, due to the influence of Mathilde and of Mme de Fervaques. But there is to be trickery within trickery, as Valenod has secretly resolved to break his promise to M. de Frilair and have Julien sentenced to death. This is an act of personal revenge because of the past rejection of his courtship by Mme de Rênal, and an act of treachery to M. de Frilair, the status of Valenod now being sufficient for him to act independently. Thus Valenod and Frilair, examples of social success achieved by clever intrigue, are portrayed as despicable specimens of humanity. By contrast, the novelist gives to his protagonist courage and generosity of character. Clearly in sympathy with his criminal hero, he places in his mouth a provocative speech to the jury which is the most fiercely political page in the novel. The bourgeois in front of me, says Julien, have no concern for justice, but only for the protection of their interests and the elimination of a class enemy:

> ... je vois des hommes qui, sans s'arrêter à ce que ma
> jeunesse peut mériter de pitié, voudront punir en moi et
> décourager à jamais cette classe de jeunes gens qui, nés
> dans un ordre inférieur et en quelque sorte opprimés par
> la pauvreté, ont le bonheur de se procurer une bonne
> éducation et l'audace de se mêler à ce que l'orgueil des
> gens riches appelle la société. (p.514)

After Stendhal's satirical portrayal of the aristocracy, a critique which is moderated by humour and some admiration, comes this fierce attack on his own class as it gladly accepts a political victim who offers himself so willingly. As chairman of this bourgeois tribunal, Valenod becomes ever more clearly a paradigm for a despicable rising class. Who is this Valenod, Mathilde asks? the reply of M. de Frilair is precise and forceful: 'C'est un parleur audacieux, impudent, grossier, fait pour mener des sots. 1814 l'a pris à la misère, et je vais en faire un préfet' (p.510). The historical significance of the character is thus firmly asserted: Valenod is an unpleasant product of the new France and a symptom of a sick society where merit counts for nothing. The penetrating M. de Frilair adds that Valenod is an example of a new 'aristocratie bourgeoise' (p.527), rich, greedy, and unscrupulous. Julien, now in prison, also asserts the power of this new class of men like Valenod: 'Ils sont bien grands en France, ils réunissent tous les avantages sociaux' (p.529). His regret is that they have none of the qualities of the declining aristocracy from which they are stealing power.

The penultimate chapter takes the form of a final assessment by Julien of human society as he has experienced it. The evaluation gradually moves from the social to the philosophical, asking fundamental questions about the human condition. The most basic relationship, that of family, is first to be observed in this disturbing chapter. Julien's last encounter with his father is placed in a symmetrical relationship with the introductory scene in which he is almost thrown into the works of the saw-mill by the paternal hand. Again the kinship is portrayed in a totally negative manner: Julien feels guilt because he has never loved his father. But he is still fearful of him, and old Sorel is portrayed as an equal of the executioner in the emotions of the protagonist, who thinks: 'Il vient au moment de ma mort me donner le dernier coup' (p.529). Despite Julien's lack of love or esteem for him, this terrible father is a judge more implacable than the one who sentences him to death. He has the power to unman his son, who briefly loses all the strength of will which had been such a feature of his character.

These paternal reproaches submit Julien to a trial more bitter and hurtful than the one which took place in the courtroom, and in which he was master of himself. In this painful scene, Julien regresses to childhood and feels a juvenile need to escape, to hide his emotions from the cruel eyes of 'ce vieillard si clairvoyant'. He eventually finds a method of self-defence in a manipulation of the old man by playing on his avarice, and Julien's conclusion is a bitter one, which extends to all paternity: 'Voilà donc l'amour de père!' (p.529). The relationship between father and son, as portrayed in Sorel and Julien, in M. de Rênal and his sons, in M. de La Mole and Norbert, ranges from hostility at worst to disappointment at best. Returning strongly in the penultimate chapter, Stendhal's obsessively negative portrayal of the relationship reveals the unhealed wounds and lingering traumas of his own distant childhood, and gives this episode a decidedly misanthropic character.

This gloomy conclusion is confirmed by the next stage in Julien's continuing reflection on social relationships. After that of censorious father and delinquent son, and possibly in an unconscious but revealing parallel, comes the relationship between citizen and criminal. In a discourse which prefigures that of Vautrin in a famous episode of *Le Père Goriot*, Julien comes to a conclusion which is a devastating criticism of those who have become rich and successful in contemporary France. The thief who narrates the story of his life to Julien stole because he was hungry, and was sent to prison by members of the bourgeoisie who have committed crimes more difficult to detect, and motivated by greed rather than need. The hero reflects that society is composed partly of those who are dishonest and rich and partly of men like his father who are not dishonest but who love only money. This thought completes his misanthropic reflection and makes him consider suicide: 'Cette philosophie pouvait être vraie, mais elle était de nature à faire désirer la mort' (p.531). Stendhal has written no page more bitter and subversive than this final evaluation of society by Julien Sorel, whose death-wish is now at its strongest. Everywhere he sees avarice, dishonesty, hypocrisy and charlatanism, and concludes sadly that humanity cannot be trusted: 'Non, l'homme ne peut pas se fier à l'homme'.

It is at this point that Julien's search for values turns briefly in the direction of religion, an orientation not often seen in one so resolute and self-sufficient. He speculates about an ideal religion which would give consolation and not be corrupted by priests. He would like to believe in God, though he cannot quite do so, and rejects the vengeful deity of the Old Testament in favour of the kind one postulated by Voltaire. But he concludes that religion cannot provide a remedy for his sense of metaphysical isolation. He reflects that his life has at least been based on a practical system which saved him from a moral void:

> Je suis isolé ici dans ce cachot; mais je n'ai pas *vécu isolé* sur la terre; j'avais la puissante idée du *devoir*. Le devoir que je m'étais prescrit, à tort ou à raison…a été comme le tronc d'un arbre solide auquel je m'appuyais pendant l'orage; je vacillais, j'étais agité. Après tout, je n'étais qu'un homme…mais je n'étais pas emporté.
>
> (p.532)

Thus Julien abandons the quest for a system of absolute values, and falls back on himself. But Stendhal brings him to one last stage in his psychological evolution, one in which this proud and egocentric cultivation of moral strength and personal duty moves towards a final affirmation of the value of sentiment.

The gradual rise of the emotional side of Julien's character is partly obscured by the narration of the details of his last days on death row and by his thoughts about society. 'En vérité, l'homme a deux êtres en lui', he had declared on an earlier occasion (p.517). In Julien is expressed a concept of the human personality as an enigma and as an arena torn by conflict. One of the competing forces which Julien now sees more clearly within himself is that of the mind and the will, a force which expresses itself in energy and ambition. The other impulse is that of feeling, which expresses itself in contemplation and passivity. It is this tendency which now becomes dominant in Julien as he responds to the devotion of Mme de Rênal and experiences a new intensity of living. He now values above all else a woman whose life was one of love, first to her children, now to him. Julien joins her children in her affections, which seem to hesitate between passion and mother-love. Her love for Julien combines passion and maternal feeling in a manner which again confirms the interest of the situation for a Freudian reading.

The motherless Julien has supplanted M. de Rênal, stern and unloved Father and symbol of authority, and found consolation in the devoted love of a maternal figure. In a final stage of his life, the condemned man has discovered how to live: 'Pour Julien, excepté dans les moments usurpés par la présence de Mathilde, il vivait d'amour et presque sans songer à l'avenir. Par un étrange effet de cette passion, quand elle est extrême et sans feinte aucune, Mme de Rênal partageait presque son insouciance et sa douce gaieté' (p.537). Julien and Mme de Rênal now see their delinquent love as a value higher than any other personal achievement. For it they have abandoned family and society. To it they sacrifice life itself, as Stendhal concludes with an affirmation of the power of passionate love to replace a world of common activities and mediocre emotions.

Sublime and Romantic transgression is thus placed above the social norm. Also true to Romantic tradition, happiness is linked to nature. When Julien walks to the guillotine, enjoying the 'sensation délicieuse' of the sun and the air, his mind full of memories of the woods of Vergy, his last wish is to be buried in the mountain cave overlooking these consoling woods. Mathilde's perversion of his request, by having the cave artificially decorated, indicates symbolically the different values of the now poetic-minded Julien and the worldly daughter of the marquis. With the death of Mme de Rênal, Stendhal grants his star-crossed lovers a sublime ending reminiscent of that of Tristan and Iseut. This conclusion has less to do with the portrayal of ordinary human behaviour than with the creation of an allegory expressing the power of love and the primacy of feeling. Social realism has given way to apotheosis. In her imitation of Marguerite de Navarre with the head of her dead lover, Mathilde is downgraded to the level of an ordinary mortal who follows in the steps of others. But in the ending given to Julien Sorel and to Mme de Rênal, Stendhal has finally satisfied his urge to portray excep-

tional characters in dramatic circumstances, and has gone beyond
realism to create two of the most striking and characteristic figures
in French Romantic literature.

Bibliographical Note

It is a paradoxical fact that the personality and ideas of Stendhal were better known a century after his death than in his own time owing to progressively improved, more complete and accessible editions of his correspondence, fragments of autobiography and diary. These personal writings have been exploited by methods inspired by psychoanalysis, one of the dominant critical approaches of our time. Examples of this are the major study by G. Blin (16), the analysis of *Le Rouge et le Noir* by Geneviève Mouillaud (10), and a stimulating study by P. Berthier (14). To these illustrations of *psychocritique* one can add the sometimes ingenious theories of J.-P. Weber (39) and of Carol Mossman (33). A second major route of approach to Stendhal is that which concentrates on historical context and examines themes such as social class and political forces. Examples of this method are provided by F.-H. Imbert (28) and by the less dependable marxist analysis of P. Barbéris (12), who claims Stendhal as a scientific materialist. Also under the historical heading there is the major study by V. del Litto (22) of the cultural influences which shaped Stendhal. A third approach to his work is seen in studies which make increasingly sophisticated use of the traditional analysis of fiction in terms of style, composition, narrative and structure. Examples of this are the studies by J. Prévost (36), V. Brombert (20), G. Blin (15), Shoshana Felman (24), and G. Genette (25). Another interesting critical method is that which gives emphasis to the reactions of readers and which can be seen in the relevant chapter in a book by C. Prendergast (35) and in recent studies of Stendhal by R. Pearson (34) and by A. Jefferson (29). I recommend also the short studies of *Le Rouge et le Noir* by P.-G. Castex (8), J. Mitchell (9), and S. Haig (11).

It is probable that some revelations made in studies inspired by psychoanalysis would have caused Stendhal surprise, even shock. Yet this is an area in which his intuition and self-examination made him a brilliant precursor and a literary phenomenon of lasting interest. Whereas the late twentieth century has seen the flourishing of new and sometimes informative critical approaches, it has also witnessed the virtual disappearance of the oldest, which was that of the moralist. It is likely that Stendhal would have urged modern readers to note that he wrote *Le Rouge et le Noir* not for psychoanalysis but to express an 'âpre vérité' about contemporary France, as he said in an epigraph. He would have added that he wrote also to entertain us, to stimulate our admiration for energy, intelligence, love and for a certain sensibility. Looking back on his childhood, the author of *Vie de Henry Brulard* (*3*, I, p.633) recalled his emotion at the age of ten when instead of doing his homework he was secretly reading Prévost's *Manon Lescaut*. He added that his furtive reading of *La Nouvelle Héloïse*, also forbidden by his parents, had made him into an 'honnête homme'. Thus emotion and virtue had come from transgression, as Prévost and Rousseau demonstrated to him both the magic of fiction and the power of a novel to propose a new morality. This important aspect of Stendhal is considered in the studies by Bourget (*19*) and Bardèche (*13*).

WORKS OF STENDHAL TO WHICH I HAVE REFERRED

1. Stendhal, *Le Rouge et le Noir*, ed. V. del Litto (Paris, Livre de Poche, 1983).
2. —, *Le Rouge et le Noir*, ed. P.-G. Castex (Paris, Bordas, 1989).
3. —, *Œuvres intimes: Journal; Vie de Henry Brulard*, ed. V. del Litto, 2 vols (Paris, Gallimard, Bibl. de la Pléiade, 1981-82).
4. —, *Correspondance*, II, ed. V. del Litto (Paris, Gallimard, Bibl. de la Pléiade, 1981–82).
5. —, *Armance* (Paris, Garnier, 1927).
6. —, *Chroniques pour l'Angleterre*, ed. K. McWatters (Université de Grenoble, 1985–).
7. —, *Vie de Rossini* (Paris, Cercle du Bibliophile, 1968).

CRITICAL WORKS: LE ROUGE ET LE NOIR

8. Castex, Pierre-Georges, *Le Rouge et le Noir de Stendhal* (Paris, SEDES, 1970).
9. Mitchell, John, *Stendhal: Le Rouge et le Noir* (London, Edward Arnold, 1973).
10. Mouillaud, Geneviève, *Le Rouge et le Noir de Stendhal* (Paris, Larousse, 1973).
11. Haig, Stirling, *Stendhal, The Red and the Black* (Cambridge University Press, 1989).
11(a). Hamm, Jean-Jacques, *Le Rouge et le Noir de Stendhal* (Paris, Gallimard, 1992).

OTHER BOOKS ON STENDHAL

12. Barbéris, Pierre, *Sur Stendhal* (Paris, Editions Sociales, 1982).
13. Bardèche, Maurice, *Stendhal romancier* (Paris, La Table Ronde,

1947).

14. Berthier, Philippe, *Stendhal et la sainte famille* (Geneva, Droz, 1983).

15. Blin, Georges, *Stendhal et les problèmes du roman* (Paris, Corti, 1958).

16. ——, *Stendhal et les problèmes de la personnalité* (Paris, Corti, 1958).

17. Bolster, Richard, *Stendhal, Balzac et le féminisme romantique* (Paris, Minard 1970).

18. ——, *Documents littéraires de l'époque romantique* (Paris, Minard, 1983).

19. Bourget, Paul, *Essais de psychologie contemporaine* (Paris, Lemerre, 1885).

20. Brombert, Victor, *Stendhal et la voie oblique* (Paris, P.U.F., 1954).

21. Crouzet, Michel, *Stendhal et le langage* (Paris, Gallimard, 1981).

22. Del Litto, Victor, *La Vie intellectuelle de Stendhal* (Paris, P.U.F., 1959).

23. Faguet, Emile, *Politiques et moralistes du dix-neuvième siècle* (Paris, Société française d'imprimerie, 1899).

24. Felman, Shoshana, *La 'Folie' dans l'œuvre romanesque de Stendhal* (Paris, Corti, 1971).

25. Genette, Gérard, *Figures* II (Paris, Seuil, 1969).

26. Hamm, Jean-Jacques, *Le Texte stendhalien* (Sherbrooke, Naaman, 1988).

27. Hemmings, F.W.J., *Stendhal: a study of his novels* (Oxford, Clarendon Press, 1964).

28. Imbert, Henri-François, *Les Métamorphoses de la liberté* (Paris, Corti, 1967).

29. Jefferson, Ann, *Reading realism in Stendhal* (Cambridge University Press, 1988).

30. Jones, Grahame, *L'Ironie dans l'œuvre de Stendhal* (Lausanne, Editions du Grand-Chêne, 1966).

31. Martineau, Henri, *L'Œuvre de Stendhal* (Paris, Le Divan, 1945).

32. McWatters, Keith, *Stendhal lecteur des romanciers anglais* (Lausanne, Editions du Grand-Chêne, 1966).

33. Mossman, Carol, *The Narrative Matrix: Stendhal's Le Rouge et le Noir* (Lexington, French Forum, 1984).

34. Pearson, Roger, *Stendhal's Violin: a novelist and his reader* (Oxford, Clarendon Press, 1988).

35. Prendergast, Christopher, *The Order of Mimesis* (Cambridge University Press, 1986).

36. Prévost, Jean, *La Création chez Stendhal* (Mercure de France, 1951).

37. Strickland, Geoffrey, *Stendhal: the education of a novelist* (Cambridge University Press, 1974).

38. Tillett, Margaret, *Stendhal, the background to the novels* (London, Oxford University Press, 1971).
39. Weber, Jean-Paul, *Stendhal: les structures thématiques de l'œuvre et du destin* (Paris, SEDES, 1969).
40. Wood, Michael, *Stendhal* (London, Elek Books, 1971).
41. Zola, Emile, *Les Romanciers naturalistes* (Paris, Charpentier, 1880).

ARTICLES AND OTHER SOURCES

42. Sainte-Beuve, *Les Grands Ecrivains français par Sainte-Beuve* (Paris, Garnier, 1927).
43. Thompson, Christopher, 'L'armée ou l'église', in *Stendhal Club*, 21, n° 83, 228–52.
44. Flaubert, *Correspondance*, II (Paris, Gallimard, Bibl. de la Pléiade, 1980).

CRITICAL GUIDES TO FRENCH TEXTS

edited by

Roger Little, Wolfgang van Emden, David Williams